THE JESUS LIBRARY

ENCOUNTERS WITH JESUS

THE JESUS LIBRARY

edited by Michael Green

ENCOUNTERS WITH JESUS

Stuart Blanch

HODDER AND STOUGHTON
LONDON SYDNEY AUCKLAND TORONTO

British Library Cataloguing in Publication Data

Blanch, Stuart Y. (Stuart Yarworth)
   Encounters with Jesus.
   1. Jesus Christ
   I. Title   II. Series
   232

   ISBN 0-340-42592-X

Dedicated to our friends and neighbours in North Oxfordshire, who have made us so much at home in their midst.

CONTENTS

EDITOR'S FOREWORD

If you have never met Dr Stuart Blanch, recently Archbishop of York, you have missed something. He is a natural leader, charming, warm, modest and humorous. He is greatly loved and rarely forgotten: his name is still cherished in Eynsham, his first parish, and in Wycliffe Hall, Oxford where he taught theology.

And all these qualities emerge unselfconsciously in this book. He is a considerable New Testament scholar. He has a profound love and respect for the New Testament documents, and not least for St Mark, the earliest gospel, on which this is an unusual type of commentary. Mark's gospel is rough, vivid, disconnected and full of the impact Jesus made on the people he met. This is the theme on which Dr Blanch has fastened. And he takes us through all the encounters people had with Jesus as recorded in this gospel. It is fascinating, as you will discover. The author knows the countryside of Palestine well, and he knows the gospel intimately. As a result he produces a book which gives an amazing depth of insight into the gospel stories. It will be invaluable to those who preach and teach the New Testament, and it will be a delight to a far wider circle of those who long to get closer to the events there recorded.

My overwhelming impression when I first read this book was one of freshness. And that is all too rare a quality in books about the New Testament, on which so much comment has been made throughout so many centuries.

Years ago Stuart Blanch came to St John's College, Nottingham, where I happened at the time to be principal. He gave some of the shrewdest talks on helping people to encounter Jesus in a personal way that I have ever heard. That same vivid shrewdness is present in this volume: it sheds a flood of light both on Jesus's own varied approach to different people, and on those whom he encounters. Enjoy it!

Michael Green

PREFACE

The Select Bibliography (Appendix A) is in itself an acknowledgment of the authors I have found particularly helpful in the latter stages of the preparation of this book. But there will be many others down the years – scholars, teachers, pupils, friends – who, without knowing it, will have contributed to my understanding of the Bible and of St Mark in particular. To them I gladly acknowledge my debt without being able to name those to whom I am thus indebted. I am especially grateful to my wife, Brenda, for transcribing from tape the original chapters, and for her constructive criticism of them in the process. And my thanks to my daughter, Angela, for producing the finished manuscript in perfect order and in good time. David Blunt, my former lay chaplain at Bishopthorpe, has added to his many kindnesses to me in being willing to read the proofs. Finally, I have to say that it has been a pleasure to work with Tim Anderson and with his colleague Andrew Hodder-Williams.

The readings at the head of each chapter are from the Holy Bible, New International Version, copyright © 1973, 1978, 1984 by International Bible Society.

INTRODUCTION

It began with an encounter. Some people came into contact with Jesus of Nazareth and stayed with him. This encounter, and what took place in the life of Jesus and in connection with his death, gave their personal lives new meaning and new significance. They felt that they had been born again, that they had been understood, and this new identity found expression in a similar solidarity towards others, their fellow-men. This change in the course of their lives was the result of their encounter with Jesus, for without him they would have remained what they had been. It had not come through any initiative of their own; it had simply happened to them. (Schillebeeckx, *Christ*, SCM 1977)

So it all began with a series of 'encounters'. There are many other ways of looking at Mark's gospel – as a prearranged series of subjects likely to be of interest to the early Church, as a manual of teaching, as a proclamation of the Pauline gospel, as a 'preacher's handbook', as a catechism or an early Church lectionary. Emboldened by Professor Schillebeeckx, I have chosen to concentrate on the encounters recorded here – not by any means all of them, but a selection, determined by the importance of the encounter either to Jesus himself or to Mark, or to the early Church. I have imposed no pattern on them, neither have I departed from the original order. They must speak for themselves, and they will speak in varying degrees of intensity to each reader. Some of them will seem far removed from present-day concerns; some of them will seem remarkably relevant, but all of them were chosen by Mark himself from the rich source of traditional material available to him. They all meant something to him, and it will be part of our task to determine more exactly what they meant.

Papias, a second-century bishop, said of the author that 'he was the interpreter of Peter, and wrote accurately, as far as he remembered them, the things said and done by him, but not, however, in order'. Marcus was a very common name in the empire, but a man named Mark did accompany Paul and Barnabas on their missionary journeys (Acts 12:25; 13:5). He proved to be a somewhat timorous missionary, and, much to Paul's annoyance, returned home when they reached Perga (Acts 13:13).

'Home' was Jerusalem, where his mother lived, and whose house served as a centre for the first Christians (Acts 12:12). We cannot prove that this Mark was the author of the gospel that bears the name. However, he is mentioned no less than eleven times in the New Testament, and it would have been a name so well known in the Church, that most readers would have assumed that it was this John Mark who had written the gospel. Who else in the early Church would have had the advantage of knowing Peter and would have travelled with Paul and Barnabas? Little else is known about him except the curious assertion that he was 'stumpy-fingered' – little else, that is to say, except that which may be deduced from the gospel he wrote.

There is a strong tradition that he wrote the gospel for the congregation at Rome. An ancient alternative is that he wrote it in Egypt, and a modern one that he wrote it in Galilee. The most likely date is in the latter half of the first century, after the outbreak of the Jewish revolt in 66 and before the fall of Jerusalem in 70. It would thus have been in the principates of Nero or Galba. As there is no way of proving authorship, date or place of composition, the reader is free to draw his own conclusions as he studies the book for himself. I shall allude to these issues more fully in the ensuing chapters.

This book is not written for experts, who are lavishly provided for already by commentaries, scholarly books and learned articles. It is intended, rather, for the reader who aspires to be a serious student of Holy Scripture, but who may lack the technical equipment needed to cope with large and intimidating books on the subject. For this reason, I have tried to make each chapter more or less self-contained. Where this leads to repetition, I crave the reader's indulgence.

I am aware of most of the important issues which have arisen in the study of the gospel over the past fifty years, but I have referred to them only when they are essential for the understanding of the text. Even so, the reader will find himself addressing his mind to some unfamiliar and complex problems. There is no easy way of penetrating the meaning of a book nearly 2,000 years old, written in an environment markedly different from our own, using thought-forms unfamiliar to us and a language in which few of my readers will be expert. I have sought only to offer a route, among many other possible, through a jungle of conflicting opinions and seeming contradictions.

But I hope the reader will be sustained by the thought that he is coming to grips with one of the most important books in the history of the world. This is a large claim, but I believe it to be justified. This gospel forms the basis of all our gospels, which remain our only reliable source of information about the life and teaching of Jesus. It is written by one who numbered among his acquaintances many of the original disciples, and accompanied Paul and Barnabas on the first official missionary journey. Thus when we read this book, however casually, we are back at the fountain-head of a movement which changed the course of history, and remains hugely influential in our attitudes to life and our understanding of the world. What we are today we are because of the events recorded in this book. No twentieth-century western man can altogether escape from this past, even if he wishes to do so. No man can altogether avoid the question – 'What do you think about the Christ?' (Matt. 22:42).

Alec McCowen attended the Lambeth Conference of 1978 and presented his famous solo act on Mark's gospel. Several of the bishops afterwards asked him whether he had been in any way influenced by his painstaking study of the book in preparation for his performances. Understandably, he gave a non-committal reply to the question. But subsequently he wrote an article for a Sunday newspaper about what it had meant to him. He ended the article, as I recall, with these words: 'Something absolutely marvellous happened in Galilee 2,000 years ago.' That is why I have written this book – to share with my readers something of the sense of wonder I felt when I first read the gospel in the RAF during the Second World War, and received my first impressions of the 'marvellous thing that happened in Galilee, 2,000 years ago'.

1

JOHN THE BAPTIST

[Mark 1:1–13]

1 The beginning of the gospel about Jesus Christ, the Son of God. [2]It is written in Isaiah the prophet:

> "I will send my messenger ahead of you,
>   who will prepare your way"—
> [3]"a voice of one calling in the desert,
>   'Prepare the way for the Lord,
>   make straight paths for him.'"

[4]And so John came, baptising in the desert region and preaching a baptism of repentance for the forgiveness of sins. [5]The whole Judean countryside and all the people of Jerusalem went out to him. Confessing their sins, they were baptised by him in the Jordan River. [6]John wore clothing made of camel's hair, with a leather belt round his waist, and he ate locusts and wild honey. [7]And this was his message: "After me will come one more powerful than I, the thongs of whose sandals I am not worthy to stoop down and untie. [8]I baptise you with water, but he will baptise you with the Holy Spirit."

[9]At that time Jesus came from Nazareth in Galilee and was baptised by John in the Jordan. [10]As Jesus was coming up out of the water, he saw heaven being torn open and the Spirit descending on him like a dove. [11]And a voice came from heaven: "You are my Son, whom I love; with you I am well pleased."

[12]At once the Spirit sent him out into the desert, [13]and he was in the desert for forty days, being tempted by Satan. He was with the wild animals, and angels attended him.

Across a featureless countryside stretches many an international boundary, marked only by a jungle of barbed wire, the occasional gun-emplacement and the arc-lights. Nothing happens for hundreds of miles, but here or there in that grim domain is a crossing-point which now and then becomes a place of high drama, a place where anxious parents await a meeting with a long-lost son or daughter, where a group of refugees take a few timid steps into a new country, where political prisoners are exchanged and pass each other with scarcely a nod or a greeting en route to home and freedom. It is a place at the same time of trembling hope and painful division.

The Jordan Valley

Such a boundary was the Jordan Valley, not then furnished with the accoutrements of modern civilisation, the barbed wire, the gun-emplacements and the arc-lights, but an important boundary nevertheless. It was far from being a serious military obstacle; the river in places is not much more than 50 feet wide, and there are numerous fords. It would hardly delay a determined enemy for more than a few hours, except in the rainy season when the river was in spate. But it had international significance. The Romans tended to regard it as a boundary between east and west, and local commanders would have been alert to any unusual movement on its banks. For Israel itself it was a place of memories. Lot, with an eye for the main chance, chose the plain of Jordan (Gen. 13), Jacob crossed the Jordan on his way to the fateful encounter with his brother Esau (Gen. 33), and it was by way of the Jordan that Joshua and his host crossed over into the Promised Land (Josh. 3). So Mark would not have regarded it as an accident that it was at the Jordan that Jesus should have met John the Baptist.

For a moment the dreary landscape is lit up: it becomes a place of high drama, the scene of a far-reaching decision that would ultimately change the course of history.

Jesus and John compared

The two men were related through their mothers. John's father was a priest and his mother was of the house of Aaron. He was born of a mother, who had been presumed barren, probably in the village of Ain Kerim, between Bethlehem and Jerusalem. He was thus a Judaean by birth in an area over which Archelaus, the older son of Herod the Great, had ruled until he was removed from power and banished by Rome. Jesus was of humbler rank altogether – of Davidic stock indeed, but no more than a humble assistant in his father's trade in the little regarded town of Nazareth in Galilee, the territory of Herod Antipas, the younger son of Herod the Great and tetrarch of Peraea and Galilee.

It is not known whether they ever met as children, and there is no record of any further meeting between them after the one recorded here. They passed, as it were, in the night – the one already a notable figure in the life of his people, with a reputation for extreme asceticism, holiness of life and fierce uncompromising speech, the other just emerging out of the hidden years and wholly unknown outside his home-town. But writing with hindsight Mark sees the inner significance of this meeting. It is the meeting of the old and the new. John was the last representative of the old prophetic order, the order which had been influential in the life of Israel for a thousand years, in his person reviving a note long since silent through the dreary centuries of exile and dispersion. He flashes across the sky and is gone.

Jesus, on the other hand, is just a local tradesman, untested by the rigours of the wilderness and the trials of public life. But in this unassuming unknown man is the beginning of something new. Later in his ministry Jesus has this to say about his older contemporary:

I tell you the truth: Among those born of women there has not risen anyone greater than John the Baptist; yet he who is least in the kingdom of heaven is greater than he. From the days of John the Baptist until now, the kingdom of heaven has been forcefully advancing, and forceful men lay hold of it. For all the Prophets and the Law prophesied until John. And if you are willing to accept it, he is the Elijah who was to come. He who has ears, let him hear.

To what can I compare this generation? They are like children sitting in the market-places and calling out to others: 'We played the flute for you, and you did not dance; we sang a dirge and you did not mourn.'

For John came neither eating nor drinking, and they say, 'He has a demon.' The Son of Man came eating and drinking, and they say, 'Here is a glutton and a drunkard, a friend of tax collectors and "sinners".' But wisdom is proved right by her actions. (Matt. 11:11–19)

What did it mean to the Church?

The encounter, however, needs to be understood not only against the background of the distant past but the background of Mark's own experience in the first century of the Church's life. The relationship between the two men as recorded in the gospels is without rancour, but there is evidence enough about tension between their disciples. They had differences of opinion about fasting (Matt. 9:14), Luke tells us that Jesus's disciples felt the need of the instruction in prayer which John had given to his disciples (Luke 11:1), and in the eyes of the Pharisees there appeared to be competition between them (John 4:1–2).

This would have been important in the early Church, because the movement which John had founded was no flash in the pan. He still had adherents in the Mediterranean world as late as the fourth century. There is evident confusion in the Acts of the Apostles about the continuing relationship between John's disciples and the Jewish members of the Christian Church (Acts 18:24–5). This is hardly surprising, because Jewish sects abounded in the first century, and it would have taken a discerning critic to make the necessary distinctions between them. The Christian group was to all appearances just another Jewish sect. So it was important for Mark's readers to know exactly what the relationship was between John and Jesus, and to observe the ready acknowledgment by John of his own subordinate role.

The point is made even more clearly in the story of John's death. In Mark's view the movement founded by John came for all practical purposes to an end when John was executed and his disciples laid his body in the tomb. The contrast could hardly have been more sharply made – John was dead and the place of his burial was known. Jesus had been dead, but was alive for evermore (Mark 6:14–29). All the references in the gospels to the relationship between John and Jesus have to be interpreted in the light of later Christian history, and that goes for many other controversial issues described in the gospels.

What did it mean to John?

We address ourselves now to the more difficult question: What did the encounter mean to the participants themselves, as distinct from what it may have meant to Mark or the early Church? Neither of them could have been wholly unaffected by this crossing-point in their lives. Let us look at John first. He was a recognisable representative of an ancient order in Israel. His dress, his habits of life and his speech were reminiscent of the great Elijah himself, who in some Jewish traditions was expected to return before the arrival of the Messiah (Mal. 4:5). Like Elijah he found his vocation in the wilderness. Not for him the comfortable suburb or the cathedral close or the king's court (Matt. 11:7–10):

> As John's disciples were leaving, Jesus began to speak to the crowd about John: "What did you go out into the desert to see? A reed swayed by the wind? If not, what did you go out to see? A man dressed in fine clothes? No, those who wear fine clothes are in kings' palaces. Then what did you go out to see? A prophet? Yes, I tell you, and more than a prophet. This is the one about whom it is written: I will send my messenger ahead of you, who will prepare your way before you."

Like the prophets of old he was concerned with the righteousness of God, and with the righteousness of the people God had chosen for his own. He had radical advice to offer to tax-collectors about how they were to conduct their business, and

warned soldiers against the acceptance of bribes. And he did
not hesitate to condemn Herod Antipas himself for his marriage to his brother's wife. It was this, according to the
gospels, that precipitated his arrest, although Josephus the
Jewish historian (AD 37–100) offers a different opinion, and it
was this that brought his meteoric public ministry to an end.
He was imprisoned in the fortress of Machaerus, and it was
there, so the gospels tell us, that he began to be assailed with
doubt about the status and mission of Jesus: 'When John
heard in prison what Christ was doing, he sent his disciples to
ask him, "Are you the one who was to come, or should we
expect someone else?"' (Matt. 11:2–3). There is nothing
either unlikely or culpable about such doubts. Many a brave
prophet, old and new, has had his doubts when isolated in
prison without any prospect of release. But long before that
he would have had cause to ponder his own ministry in
relation to that of Jesus:

> To this John replied, "A man can receive only what is given him
> from heaven. You yourselves can testify that I said, 'I am not the
> Christ but am sent ahead of him.' The bride belongs to the
> bridegroom. The friend who attends the bridegroom waits and
> listens for him, and is full of joy when he hears the bridegroom's
> voice. That joy is mine, and it is now complete. He must become
> greater; I must become less." (John 3:27–30)

For him the arrival of his kinsman in the crowd by the River
Jordan was a moment of joyous recognition, but it was also a
moment of radical challenge to his own vocation as a prophet
of God. He knew in his bones that he would have to grow less,
that his heyday was over, that his work was complete. It could
not have been evident to the onlookers, but it was inevitable.
They would pass in the night, he into obscurity, Jesus into the
full light of the coming day. It was a significant crossing-point
in the history of mankind.

What did it mean to Jesus?

What did the encounter mean to Jesus, emerging out of the shadows of the hidden years? He would presumably have already seen in John, his kinsman, a genuine prophet of God reviving in his life style and manner of speech the memories of a former age. He would have identified in him the authentic proclamation of the coming Kingdom of God, and would, with many others, have been excited and elated by it. Something in his past now prepared him for what he was about to do next. He did nothing more in the first instance than join himself to the crowd which gathered round John, listening not only to the words, but to the Word of God to him, in what he perceived to be a critical moment in his own life.

In accordance with Mark's usual style, the baptism of Jesus is recorded without comment, but it was obviously a problem to the early Church, and Matthew offers a kind of explanation in the words of John – ' "I need to be baptised by you, and do you come to me?" ' (Matt. 3:14). Of course it was a problem, given the development of doctrine in the first century, and the ascending honour in which Jesus was held. How could it be that he, the sinless son of God, should have to pass through the waters of baptism? But that was to read too much altogether into the incident. Baptism was a distinctive, even singular, feature of John's ministry; no previous prophet had engaged in it. But it was not without precedent in the life of Israel. Preoccupied as the orthodox Jew was with ritual cleansing, washing had long played a part in temple worship and domestic piety. Moreover, it had long been the ritual association with the reception of a proselyte to the Jewish faith. In that sense it would have been extremely offensive to the devout Jew to undergo such a ceremony as if he were numbered among the Gentiles. But the rite of baptism would have been more likely to have been associated in the minds of those who underwent it with the dawning of the promised Messianic age.

Ezekiel had spoken of the time when God would 'sprinkle clean water upon you and you would be clean' (Ezek. 36:25). Zechariah had prophesied the time when God would open a

fountain to the house of David and the inhabitants of Jerusalem (Zech. 13:1). So in a word (the preaching of the
Kingdom) and in deed (the administration of baptism), John
was fulfilling a long-held belief in the coming of the Messianic
age. It was probably this aspect of baptism which dominated
Jesus's understanding and led him to be baptised himself.
Something in his own past had prepared him for it; he had
identified in the ministry of John the moment of truth for
himself. He stood at the crossing between the old and the
new, and received an inner assurance of his stupendous
vocation, transcending anything that his kinsman John had
ever envisaged.

The voice of God

Luke's account of the Baptism (Luke 3:21–3) suggests that it
was an experience shared by the bystanders. But that is not
the sense of Mark's account. It was Jesus alone who saw
heaven opened and the Spirit descending on him like a dove.
It was Jesus alone, not the others, who heard the voice from
heaven. The voice from heaven was a familiar feature of
Hebrew history. Abraham had heard it in Haran (Gen. 12),
Moses heard it at Sinai (Exod. 19:19). Elijah heard it at the
mouth of the cave at Horeb (1 Kgs. 19:12). Isaiah heard it in
the Temple (Isa. 6:8). Ezekiel heard it by the banks of the
River Kebar among the exiles of Babylon (Ezek. 1:24). St
Paul heard it on the road to Damascus (Acts 26:14). So Jesus
as a student of sacred Scriptures would not have been unfamiliar with the idea of the voice of God from heaven, and
not altogether unprepared for it. But it needs to be observed
that in every case described above the voice from heaven was
associated with mission: it constituted a summons to a task. In
Mark's view Jesus's baptism in the River Jordan did not call
for explanation; it marked the beginning of Jesus's mission
which he is about to describe. It was 'The beginning of the
gospel about Jesus Christ the son of God' (v. 1).

2

THE FISHERMEN

[Mark 1:14–22]

[14]After John was put in prison, Jesus went into Galilee, proclaiming the good news of God. [55]"The time has come," he said. "The kingdom of God is near. Repent and believe the good news!"

[16]As Jesus walked beside the Sea of Galilee, he saw Simon and his brother Andrew casting a net into the lake, for they were fishermen. [17]"Come, follow me," Jesus said, "and I will make you fishers of men." [18]At once they left their nets and followed him.

[19]When he had gone a little farther, he saw James son of Zebedee and his brother John in a boat, preparing their nets. [20]Without delay he called them, and they left their father Zebedee in the boat with the hired men and followed him.

[21]They went to Capernaum, and when the Sabbath came, Jesus went into the synagogue and began to teach.[22] The people were amazed at his teaching, because he taught them as one who had authority, not as the teachers of the law.

One of the difficulties of arriving at a proper estimate of Mark's gospel is the difficulty of isolating it from other gospels with which we are familiar. Unconsciously we import into our reading of it other information derived from Matthew, Luke and John. We thus deprive ourselves of the freshness and clarity of this gospel, which in the view of most scholars is the first one to have been written, and therefore occupies a unique position for the understanding of Jesus himself, of the author and of the Church for which the gospel was written. This difficulty is never more real than in this primitive account of the call of the first disciples.

Luke and John

It may seem a perverse way of making the point, but it might
help the reader if I outline features of the call which we owe to
the other evangelists, and which therefore have to be ignored
if we are to understand Mark in his own right. Matthew
(4:18–22) follows Mark closely and supplies nothing extra.
Luke (5:1–11) obviously draws on other resources and en-
larges the narrative. In his case Jesus uses Simon's boat as a
kind of sea-going pulpit, from which he speaks to the crowd
that has assembled on the shore. When he has finished
speaking he suggests that Simon should let down his net for a
draught. Simon, a seasoned fisherman, not unnaturally de-
murs. After all, if they had been fishing all night and had
caught nothing it was unlikely that they would catch anything
in broad daylight. But he agrees and lets down the net. The
catch is so large that he has to summon help from his partners
in the other boat, and both boats begin to sink with the
weight. Simon is overcome with fear, confesses himself a
sinful man, and Jesus calls him and his partners, James and
John, to 'catch men'. Andrew is not mentioned by name at
all.

John (1:29–51) has no exact parallel. In his case, the call of
the first disciples takes place 'beyond Jordan where John was
baptising'. John the Baptist is standing with two of his disciples when Jesus passes by, and witnesses to him as 'the
Lamb of God'. One of the two is Andrew, who then proceeds
to find his brother Simon. The other disciple who had been
standing with John the Baptist is unnamed.

Luke and John therefore offer variant accounts of the call
of the first disciples, and no amount of ingenuity can
altogether reconcile them. But that for the moment is not the
point. The point to note is that the call of the disciples in Mark
is strikingly bare when we no longer supply material from the
other evangelists. No attention is paid to the circumstances of
the call, or to the state of mind of the four fishermen, so
dramatically uprooted from their previous way of life. We
shall have cause to observe Mark's aptitude for understate-
ment elsewhere in our study of the gospel. And it will make us

aware how much we owe to the later evangelists for so much that we take for granted.

This encounter with the fishermen is on any reckoning one of the most important events in the life of Jesus, and was to be of enormous significance in the history of the Apostolic Church. Yet it is recounted in five sentences, with no description of the scene, with no information about the four fishermen, with no reason given for their swift and unquestioning response, and with no suggestion that these men were ultimately to be 'pillars of the Church', to which Mark and his readers belonged. This is all the more surprising if, as is often supposed, Mark is indebted to one of the four, Peter, for much of the material he has assembled in the gospel. Did not Peter remember what happened on what would have seemed to most of us a never-to-be-forgotten day? Did he have nothing to say about the circumstances under which he first met the Lord of Life? Did he give no impression of the excitement which the encounter generated in his mind? Could he not recover that sense of wonder which caused him to leave his chosen profession and follow without delay? The account is more remarkable for what it leaves out than for what it includes. This calls for explanation and I hope this study will go some way at least to providing it.

Mark's sources of information

Meanwhile, however, we have to allow for the fact that Mark was not writing as a modern reporter with facts not already known to his readers. Such facts as Mark had at his disposal were derived from an already existing tradition in the Church to which he belonged. In the early Church there was no 'New Testament' to which they could refer. They may have had in their possession a few letters from revered members of the Church like James or Paul. Otherwise their only Bible was the Greek version of the Hebrew Old Testament, which in their view prefigured the life of Christ, but certainly did not describe it. So for information about Jesus they had to rely on the oral testimony of those who had known him in the flesh or were in some way associated with those who had known him. If the gospel was written as is generally believed before the fall of Jerusalem in AD 70, there could well have been members of the congregation who had first-hand acquaintance with one of the early disciples. There were after all 500 of them to whom Jesus appeared after his resurrection (1 Cor. 15:6), some of whom could still have been alive. Mark, therefore, in addition to any material he may have received from Peter, would have had access to this general fund of knowledge. He is not writing to communicate the wholly unknown; he is more of a commentator than a reporter, and does not feel any need to elaborate on incidents in Jesus's life, which would already be familiar to his readers.

It could be that the gospels arose, or at least took their present form, at a time when the numbers who had any first-hand knowledge of Jesus were fast diminishing, and the Church began to feel its need for a reliable account of what really happened forty years ago in Galilee and Jerusalem. The material in the other gospels which is additional to Mark could have been relying on traditions which were not available to Mark. Variations in narrative between the gospels, of which there are many, could have been caused by a different principle of selection or by variant traditions which grew up separately in widely separated parts of the Christian Church. There is nothing mysterious or disturbing about the growth of such variant traditions: this is the way in which most ancient literature, Hebrew, Christian or Greek, achieved the forms in which we now know it.

Mark's Purpose

The brevity of Mark's account may owe something to two other factors. We do not know who Mark was, though I see no reason to dispute the long-held opinion that it was in his mother's house in Jerusalem that Jesus and his disciples met for their last supper, and that he subsequently became the companion of Paul and Barnabas on their missionary journeys. If he was writing for a Roman congregation he would be writing largely for people who had never been to Palestine and would be wholly ignorant of the geography of the land in which the events described took place. There was no point, therefore, in providing elaborate settings for the events described. I have myself been to Israel many times and I have academic aids at my elbow. Even so I should be hard pressed to grasp in detail the various travel sections of the gospel and present them to you, the reader. The Greek slave, the Roman officer, the Syrian merchant in the congregation in Rome, could hardly be expected to wrestle with such details.

The other factor not so obvious to us, with our high speed transport, is that Mark was a native of Jerusalem, and may never have been to Galilee in his life. Why should he? It was seventy-five miles away, even taking the direct route through Samaria, which was commonly avoided by Jewish travellers. The events he was recording in Galilee took place when he was little more than a child, and such contact as he may have had with Jesus and his disciples was limited to their occasional visits to Jerusalem for the festivals. There were no maps to be had at the local newsagent. Therefore, to him the place names, to which the disciples may from time to time have referred, would have been meaningless. Capernaum, Nazareth, Bethsaida, Caesarea, would have been just names to him, their geographical relationship with each other quite unknown. So the kind of material to which a modern biographer has access was not available to Mark. It would be as difficult to write a connected history of Christ as it would be for a mid-West American to write convincingly about Gandhi, having never met him or visited India.

Whatever else Mark's gospel may be it is not in our sense of the word a biography – and does not claim to be. For whatever reasons Mark may have written this was not one of them, and it will be one of the aims of this study to try to uncover what his intention was. Under what impulse of the Spirit did he write? To what issue in the life of the early Church was he addressing himself? What was his attitude to the disciples of Jesus so summarily mentioned at this point in the narrative? It is a cardinal principle of the study of any book of the Bible to ask such questions. Ancient writers did not have publishers to encourage them; they did not write for profit or, with some exceptions, for fame. Presumably they did not write just for their own amusement.

The fact that we need to make a sharp distinction between what is actually in the gospel and what we unconsciously import into it from other sources ought not to inhibit us from making use of those other resources if they supplement or illuminate the narrative we have in front of us. Thus, Mark makes no room in his gospel for the miraculous draught of fishes recorded by Luke, but at least Luke offers supportive evidence for the fact that the encounter did take place on the shores of the Sea of Galilee. Similarly Mark makes no room for the calling of the first disciples at the River Jordan, but it is not unreasonable to suppose that John is right in suggesting that the first disciples of Jesus had originally been disciples of John the Baptist. Mark at least permits that association when he says that it was 'After John was put into prison, Jesus went into Galilee, proclaiming the good news of God' (v. 14). Given that Jesus was baptised by John, no doubt in company with many others from Galilee, it would not be surprising if some of his companions, stunned by the news of John's arrest, transferred their allegiance to Jesus. On this basis it looks as if Jesus, after his baptism and temptation, returned to Galilee and there in the course of time renewed his former acquaintance with the four fishermen. It was to be in Galilee, with Galilean disciples, that he was to achieve his greatest public success, and it was to Galilee, according to Mark, that he was to return after his resurrection.

Galilee

It is important to have some knowledge of Galilee if we are to account for his striking success there. Busy pilgrims today, exhausted by a hectic schedule in Jerusalem, often remark on the sense of peace that overtakes them when they reach Galilee and look out across the tranquil waters of the lake to the mountains beyond. But that experience could be misleading. In the early years of the first century Judea was a backwater; Galilee was the centre of a humming political and commercial life. It stood at the crossroads of the nations of the ancient world, through which the armies and the traders and the diplomats passed. There some of the greatest battles of the world had been fought. Jerusalem had the reputation for a narrow piety based on the Temple. Galilee was the home of a thoroughly cosmopolitan population: Greek, Hebrew and Aramaic would all be heard in the markets; Syrian, Jew, Roman and Parthian mixed freely. It was a land of passing excitements and dangerous fashions, of a barbarous dialect and offensive manners.

The political scene

The political scenery of Galilee is every bit as important as the natural scenery for our understanding of Jesus's ministry there. The history of the area is notoriously difficult to grasp and even more difficult to communicate when it is grasped. For our purpose, however, we need to be familiar just with the following facts. Herod the Great, who was king of Judea when Jesus was born, was married ten times and had fourteen children, nine sons and five daughters. Three of his sons had been put to death on his own orders. The oldest surviving son was only 18 when Herod died. In Herod's will he was to be king, but only of Judea and Samaria. Antipas, another son, was to inherit Galilee and Peraea, and Philip was to inherit the north-east territories at the foot of Mount Hermon. When Jesus's ministry began in Galilee, Archelaus had already been banished for misrule, leaving Judea and Samaria under the direct rule of Rome. Antipas still reigned in Galilee and Peraea ('that fox' as Jesus called him). These political divisions were to be of some significance for Jesus himself, but the hard fact was that whether by direct rule or rule by puppet leaders it was Rome that held the strings of power in an area which served as a useful buffer against the marauding peoples of the east. History tends to repeat itself. The inhabitants of Galilee, and Jesus among them, lived in what was in effect a subject land. Evidences of foreign rule were all around them –

the barracks, the court-house, the official state buildings; they were inured to the sound of the lash and the cry of the patriot as he hung upon a Roman cross. When, therefore, Jesus spoke to the Twelve about taking up their cross, he was not speaking figuratively as we are apt to suppose; he was speaking of a real potential danger to which all his countrymen were sometimes exposed.

The Religious Scene

The religious scenery is even more important than the natural or political scenery for the understanding of Jesus's success in the land. Substantial Jewish settlement in the area was of comparatively recent origin, and the Jewish settlers were painfully conscious of the threat to their faith implicit in the bubbling, exciting Greek-style life which lay all around them. They had their own synagogues, but the younger generation felt the pull of the Greek gymnasium and the Greek theatre and the Greek hippodrome. They even wanted to wear their hair short like their Greek contemporaries. They had the sacred Scriptures, but there were other books around which offered a somewhat different way of life and proposed somewhat different objectives. So in Galilee the Jews were at risk, and as invariably happens in such circumstances, they developed a certain sort of fanaticism. They were regarded by the Judeans as unorthodox, but they were enthusiasts, quick to respond to the latest charismatic figure, ready to identify a new Messiah. Because perhaps of their exposure to Roman imperial might, they eagerly looked forward to the day when they would once more have a king of their own – if not next week, at the end of the age. They were an excitable people, prone to act first and think afterwards, and it was not difficult to 'rent a crowd'. It was in such a land and under such conditions that Jesus began his ministry.

The first disciples

Mark, unlike Luke, offers no explanation for the fishermen's immediate response to Jesus's invitation. Jesus came, he saw, he called. It is typical of the gospel as a whole that everything happens at top speed. The word for 'immediately' occurs forty-two times, with which compare Matthew seventeen times and Luke seven times, both of them much longer than Mark. But perhaps there is a clue to that 'immediate' response in the way in which this first chapter is organised. A modern Bible has to be divided into chapters and paragraphs and verses, but they are not, of course, original to the text and they can be misleading. For example, the last two verses at the end of the passage are normally treated as part of the next section, but they may offer a clue to Mark's understanding of the call of the fishermen. If so there is a hint, no more, as to what it was which first drew the fishermen to Jesus. It was the same power as that which first drew the crowds: viz., the sheer authority of his teaching. In any case it has to be said that the reaction of the fishermen was not so extraordinary as it seems to us. Whatever the forceful impact on us of another person, we should be unlikely at the drop of a hat to decide not to go to work that day or to quit our profession or to leave wife and children.

The Galileans were less cautious. It was not unknown for would-be disciples to attach themselves to a famous rabbi, not just to hear a course of lectures or attend evening classes, but to live with him and travel together, absorbing not only his words but his life style. It was not uncommon for there to be twelve such followers in one group, not because twelve was considered to be an optimum figure, but because it symbolised the hope that one day the kingdom of Israel would once again be established on the basis of the original twelve tribes of Israel. Such groups did not usually achieve permanence, and their membership varied with changing circumstance or fluctuating enthusiasm. This is reflected in John 6:67 – 'will ye also go away?' (AV).

Jesus's group was different from others in at least two ways. They did stay together for as long as three years, and they did not choose him; he chose them. So the relationship between Jesus and the disciples was not an unfamiliar one in the ancient world, nor was the encounter as dramatic as preachers sometimes suggest. Nevertheless, it took something special for these men to leave their nets and become part of this new group. It is possible, as we have seen, that they may have been influenced by John the Baptist and may indeed have been his disciples. There may have been intimations from the Baptist himself about the role of Jesus as his successor. But clearly, whatever other motives were at work, they had come under the spell of one who spoke with authority and proclaimed that the Kingdom of God was near. Any Galilean would prick up his ears at a message about the coming of the Kingdom of God, even if he saw in it only an alternative to the detested Roman rule. Indeed, even when their apprenticeship was nearly complete the disciples were still asking the same old question as to when the kingdom would be restored to Israel (Acts 1:6). Those old hopes of national independence and freedom from foreign power died hard, and even Jesus's closest followers never altogether extricated themselves from them. These fishermen had a lot to learn from their new rabbi.

It is necessary to observe that at this stage the relationship between Jesus and his disciples was not that of a divine being or a supernatural person with devout worshippers, but the more homely and familiar relationship between the gifted teacher and his eager pupils. Just as we have to disabuse ourselves of notions acquired from other gospels, we have to be careful not to read into the gospel narrative attitudes and relationships which are the later product of Christian history and theology. The man they encountered by the Sea of Galilee that day was a young man, younger perhaps than they were, who had been brought up in Nazareth only 20 miles away, who had had only an elementary education in the synagogue school, who yet exhibited in their eyes an air of unmistakable authority and learning. Furthermore, he was bringing them 'good news of God'.

Discipleship

The remarkable brevity of Mark's account of what seems to us
a highly important moment in the life of Jesus and subsequently of the Church may betray his view of the role and
status of the disciples. In this connection the Venerable Bede
(673–735) makes a good point when he says – 'now fishers and
unlettered men are sent to preach, that the faith of believers
might be thought to lie in the power of God, not in eloquence
or learning'. He was not the first nor would be the last to make
that point. For example, Mark's mentor, Paul of Tarsus,
reminded his readers that:

> Brothers, think of what you were when you were called. Not
> many of you were wise by human standards; not many were
> influential; not many were of noble birth. But God chose the
> foolish things of the world to shame the wise; God chose the weak
> things of the world to shame the strong. He chose the lowly things
> of this world and the despised things – and the things that are not
> – to nullify the things that are, so that no-one may boast before
> him. (1 Cor. 1:26–9)

'So be it,' Mark is saying, 'that is how it is.' The twelve
disciples, later to be called apostles, did not owe their place in
the Church to their natural virtues or their natural strength,
but to the fact that they had been called, and had obeyed.
That is what discipleship means – everywhere and at all times.

3

THE CALLING OF LEVI

[Mark 2:13–17]

[13]Once again Jesus went out beside the lake. A large crowd came to him, and he began to teach them. [14]As he walked along, he saw Levi son of Alphaeus sitting at the tax collector's booth. "Follow me," Jesus told him, and Levi got up and followed him.

[15]While Jesus was having dinner at Levi's house, many tax collectors and "sinners" were eating with him and his disciples, for there were many who followed him. [16]When the teachers of the law who were Pharisees saw him eating with the "sinners" and tax collectors, they asked his disciples: "Why does he eat with tax collectors and 'sinners'?"

[17]On hearing this, Jesus said to them, "It is not the healthy who need a doctor, but the sick. I have not come to call the righteous, but sinners."

Between the calling of the first disciples Simon, Andrew, James and John and the calling of Levi there was a period of days or weeks of intense, not to say feverish, activity. Jesus and his new disciples went first to Capernaum, a town on the lakeside which seems to have become a more or less permanent base for his ministry in Galilee. They went to the town synagogue and there encountered a man with an evil spirit who, to the astonishment of the congregation, was healed by Jesus. As soon as they left the synagogue they went to Simon's home where Simon's mother-in-law was in bed with a fever. Jesus took her by the hand and helped her up, and the fever left her. The same evening, after sunset, when the Sabbath was over and people were free to travel again, crowds of people from the town gathered at the door of the house. Jesus, it is said, healed many who had various diseases and drove out many demons.

The following morning he got up early, left the house, and went off to a solitary place for prayer. But Simon and his companions, not unnaturally excited by the events of the previous day, cannot wait for further demonstrations of his power to heal, and pursue him into the hills. So he travelled throughout Galilee preaching in their synagogues and driving out demons. It is often said with some justice that this narrative of the first day is intended as a kind of sample of Jesus's life and ministry from that time onwards – pursued by the crowds, taxed by the demands of the physically sick and the mentally disturbed, having to extract himself to make some time alone with God free from the attentions of the people, and accompanied by a rather excited little group of disciples eager to share in the sudden popularity of their Master.

Conflict Stories (Mark 1:40–3:6)

There follows a series of what are often called 'conflict stories', because they are concerned not so much with acts of healing, but with the opposition to those acts of healing engendered among the official representatives of Judaism. Jesus touches a man with leprosy, whereas the Law was that such a man should be banned from any contact with the public. Then he heals a paralysed man and associates that healing with the forgiveness of sins; this was an offence to his opponents because in their view God alone could forgive sins.

In the same series of encounters there is a dispute with John the Baptist's disciples and the Pharisees about fasting, followed by an argument about the keeping of the Sabbath when Jesus, going through the cornfields, allowed his disciples to pick some ears of corn, which was forbidden on the Sabbath. A similar dispute arose about a man with a withered hand who was healed by Jesus on the Sabbath – which, in the view of his opponents, again was contrary to the Law.

It is in the context of these conflict stories that the call of Levi is placed. This raises two issues of which we need to be aware. The first, a general one which applies to all study of the Scriptures, is that the understanding of the context of any event or saying is absolutely crucial to its proper interpretation. We would have been saved a lot of extravagances and misunderstandings if that rule had always been observed. The second issue is connected with the literary form of the gospel. With some notable exceptions there is no attempt to provide a rigid, chronological framework. Sometimes events are recorded in the order of their happening, but often on the basis of their common theme. This is particularly important here because the call of Levi occurs in a series of conflict stories and is thus not to be understood in the same way as the calling of Peter, Andrew, James and John.

The importance of Levi in the author's mind was that it created yet another conflict with the leaders of the Jewish religion. To them a tax-collector was a 'sinner' by virtue of his occupation, and it was unthinkable that a zealous orthodox Jew would associate with him. The call of Levi is not just an event, it is a symbol, a symbol of the radical difference between the religion of Jesus and the religion of his opponents which was to be a source of conflict with them throughout his ministry. One of the most persistent criticisms of him was that he had 'unfortunate' friends.

The tax man

In the world today a tax-collector is hardly a popular figure, but he is not quarantined: he is seen to be a necessary, and indeed an indispensable, agent of government, providing the revenue which a modern state requires for defence, health and social services, education and transport. This was true also of the Roman state, but it was not obvious to the tax-payers of an imperial dependency in Palestine that the taxes so gathered were for their own good. In their view the tax system was designed to further Rome's imperial ambitions, and to provide for the vast bureaucracy of empire centred in Rome. They got nothing back in terms of health services, education or local roads. The great highways existed for the rapid movement of Roman legionaries, not for the benefit of the local resident or the local trader.

There was a whole network of taxes designed to extract maximum income from the tributary nations. There was the tribute money which had to be paid in Roman coinage, bearing the effigy of the Roman emperor; that in itself was an offence to the Jewish mind. And then there were annual contributions in corn and cattle which went to help feed the Roman troops. And then there were sales taxes and custom duties. And the whole edifice was administered by 'publicans', often men of great wealth and weight in the local community.

Levi was not one of the great publicans, but a minor official in Capernaum or what we would call today a customs officer. His unpopularity would not have derived only from his profession but from the fact that his profession was exercised in the employment of the much-despised Herod Antipas, the tetrarch of Galilee and Peraea, who would be out to gather as much as he could from his tiny kingdom. And where better than in Capernaum? It was on the border of his territory, through which goods passed in abundance not only from his brother's territory, Philip the tetrarch, but from the Greek cities of the Decapolis.

Levi, therefore, although technically employed by Herod, would be widely recognised as being an agent of the imperial system, a traitor to the Jewish people, and a renegade from the Law of God. It could hardly be otherwise. He mixed on equal terms with Gentiles and Greeks and Syrians, shared in their meals, used common vessels and, worst of all, disregarded the Sabbath. On the whole Jewish susceptibilities were honoured by the Romans, but business did not stop on the Sabbath in Galilee, and the customs house would still have to be open. So the calling of Levi is a 'conflict story' in the sense that in calling such a man Jesus exposed himself to the charge that he sat too easily to the Law, that he was failing to sustain the Jewish community in its religious and social

solidarity and compromising their deep-felt opposition to
foreign rule.

As in many societies before and since, those who aspire to
religious leadership are expected to take seriously the political and social aspirations of their people. Even the other four
disciples may well have been startled by this unwelcome
addition to their ranks. Were they expected to treat this
tarnished newcomer as one of themselves? By the time the
apostolic band was complete, they were to have some very
odd companions. One of them, for example, was a rabid
nationalist, a member of the Zealot party, who would have
been violently opposed to the rule of Rome, and would have
stopped at nothing, like a modern terrorist, to challenge it. If
the call of Levi offended the Jews, the call of Simon the Zealot
would certainly have alarmed Herod and his masters in
Rome.

The priority of Mark

This brings us to another issue, the priority of Mark's gospel
(Mark 3:13–19). The name of Levi does not occur, but
Matthew's list of the apostles (Matt. 10:1–4) does include a
tax-collector, whose name is Matthew. It is true that Jewish
children often did acquire other names. Jesus himself gave
Simon another name – Peter; he nicknamed James and John
'Boanerges', which means 'sons of thunder', but the identification of Levi the tax-collector with Matthew the tax-
collector is by no means certain.

One of the earliest biblical scholars in the Church, Origen
(185–254) asserted that Levi was not of the number of the
apostles; the issue has been argued ever since without producing an unqualified answer. The issue is not of any great
importance except insofar as the identification of Levi with
Matthew did have curious results subsequently in the relative
importance ascribed to the gospels. Matthew's gospel
achieved a priority in the early Church because it was largely
believed that it was the only gospel which had direct apostolic
authority. There is no claim by the authors of Mark, Luke or

John that they were members of the apostolic band. If the association of Levi with Matthew is accepted then his gospel stands alone as a direct link with the life and ministry of Jesus. The most, however, that we can safely say is that the early writers of the Church believed that the gospel according to Matthew did include material written in Aramaic which was believed to have been derived from Matthew the tax-collector. Whoever was responsible for the final form of Matthew's gospel as we know it was almost certainly not a member of the apostolic band – and this for good reasons which most modern New Testament scholars accept.

Mark's gospel appears to be the basic document upon which both Matthew and Luke are based; they follow roughly his order of events, sometimes they import his text totally into their own manuscripts, and where they depart from him they depart either on the grounds of correcting, as they believe, an error or giving a different interpretation of it. If the author of Matthew had been, as Mark was certainly not, a member of the apostolic band, he would have been better equipped than Mark to construct his own narrative based on personal reminiscence.

The importance of this seeming digression is to establish the priority of the gospel with which we are now concerned. It is basic to the other gospels and it is the earliest record we have of the life and teaching of Christ, written by someone who though not himself a member of the apostolic band was closely in touch with some who were. As we read this gospel we are back to the fountain-head of the Christian faith and the Christian Church, and we have to try to read it without the qualifications, the contradictions, the interpretations which we acquire unconsciously from the other gospels. For my part I believe that we can identify Matthew with Levi, and that we may owe to him indirectly some valuable elements which later became part of the gospel which we know by his name. More than that can hardly be said.

The Apostles

The call of Levi exposes a feature of the apostolic band with which we may not be familiar, and to this I now turn. The apostles occupy an honoured and prominent place in the life and history of the Church. Churches are dedicated to them, stained-glass windows are designed in their honour, the calendar gives each of them a day in the Christian year and provides suitable lections for them. In the development of Christian doctrine furious argument has raged from time to time about the nature of their office and the extent to which that office is continued in the life of the Church. The meaning of the 'Apostolic Succession' remains, after centuries of debate, a burning issue in ecumenical relationships. Their symbolic importance is undoubted, but the strange fact is that we know little about them.

No further 'call' is recorded in Mark until a list of the apostles appears in Mark 3:13–19. The list itself is not unambiguous, but there is a wide measure of accord about who constituted the apostolic band. We know that the first disciples were fishermen, the fifth disciple was a tax-collector, and we know that one of them was a Zealot. Information about the rest is wholly lacking except for the unhappy Judas, whose fate is well chronicled. They appear corporately as 'the Twelve', and they are on stage in the gospel as a corporate body from beginning to end.

They are not given a good press: they are shown severally or together as obtuse, impetuous, naïve, cowardly and treacherous. It is such men as these that we honour in our stained-glass windows and intone their names on great ecclesiastical occasions. Furthermore, their subsequent history in the Church does little to restore their lustre. They are mentioned as a body in the early part of the Acts of the Apostles, e.g. Acts 1:13–14; they witness bravely to the resurrection, they are the centre of an enthusiastic and swiftly-growing movement in Jerusalem. Thereafter they gradually drop out of view. James died a martyr's death in AD 44, John is mentioned, but no more, in Galatians 2:9 (AD 52 or 56). Peter is prominent in the early days of the Church but yields in importance to James, the Lord's brother, and is heard of no more after Acts 15. The effective leadership in Palestine is vested in James, who was certainly not a member of the Twelve, and, in the dispersion, in Paul.

Legends abound about the later activities of the apostles and their worldwide mission, but within the Scriptures themselves they do not seem to play a significant part once they have fulfilled their primary function as witnesses to the resurrection. Given the likely fact that Mark was writing some time between AD 66 and 70, we are bound to ask what role in his view they played more than as a group of pupils gathered round their rabbi. After all, by the late sixties some of them – even if they had been young men when they met Jesus – would have died, and most of them would have been quite unknown to the congregation for which Mark was writing. They would have known about Paul, even Peter, but of the rest they would know nothing.

Our response to these facts is bound to influence our interpretation of the gospel as a whole. There was a time in my own career as a teacher when I confidently taught that the apostles were the central theme of the gospel – how they had been called, how they had been taught, how they had been prepared for apostolic ministry. Like many of my previous opinions I have had to abandon it; the gospel will not bear the weight of such an interpretation given their low profile in the Church of Mark's day. In Mark's gospel they are simply 'around' – to give such companionship and to do such tasks as were necessary for Jesus himself.

Their vital role was to be witnesses of the resurrection, a role which they courageously fulfilled. They provided the essential link between the Jesus of Nazareth on earth and the Lord of glory in heaven; the Son of God really had lived on earth, had eaten and drunk and joked with his disciples, and they knew beyond all peradventure that he was the man who was crucified on Good Friday, buried on Good Friday evening, and rose triumphant from the tomb the following Sunday morning. Jesus was no ghost or phantom as some opponents of the Christian Church alleged, but a real man – and they had been his companions for three years.

We do right to honour them because they did the job they were called to do with enthusiasm and courage and there was no more that they could do, but perhaps in Mark's mind the Twelve had what we might call an exemplary role as well. He had, after all, been an assistant to Paul, and he would have learnt from him that not many wise or good or rich or well-endowed were necessarily called to the service of Christ. There could hardly be a better example of that truth than in the constitution of the apostolic band. They were not, by any standards, exceptional people. They are revealed in all their unimpressive humanity in the gospel – obtuse, impetuous, naïve, cowardly – this is how they were most of the time, and in the longer ending of St Mark's gospel they are berated for their unbelief (Mark 16:14).

Yet they had in common one virtue which ranked above all others in Mark's mind, and maybe in the Church at large – they saw it through, they stuck it out, they proved their ultimate devotion to Christ in the distresses they suffered and the risks they took. They proved to be 'martyrs', i.e. witnesses to an essential, life-changing, world-renewing event. That, Mark is saying to his congregation, is the mark of the real Christian disciple – not learning, social prestige, gracious manners, physical hardihood or courage, but – to use a modern expression – stickability.

Mark was writing at a time of great disturbance in the world, with the Jewish revolt under way in Palestine, with the detested Nero on the throne of the empire, with three short-lived emperors to follow him. The foundations of a great civilisation seemed to be moving. In such an atmosphere anything could happen – and some Christians certainly paid the price of their allegiance to Christ, and some no doubt also concealed or denied their faith under the threat of persecution.

At such a time they could at least, Mark said, look back to the example of the apostles. The message of Mark is the message of the writer to the Hebrews – under these conditions: 'Let us fix our eyes on Jesus, the author and perfecter of our faith, who for the joy set before him endured the cross, scorning its shame, and sat down at the right hand of the

throne of God. Consider him who endured such opposition
from sinful men, so that you will not grow weary and lose
heart' (Heb. 12:2–3).

Two views of religion

The call of Levi is a 'conflict story'. On the surface it is a
conflict between Jesus and his opponents, about relationships
with those who were despised and discredited members of the
Jewish community, excluded from Israel by virtue of their
occupation or of their inability to keep the Law. In the eyes of
the Pharisees all such were 'sinners', and it was a recurring
complaint that Jesus spent far too much time with such
sinners. His answer, one which has brought comfort and
strength and hope to many another since Levi, is: 'It is not the
healthy who need a doctor, but the sick. I have not come to
call the righteous, but sinners' (Mark 2:17).

But beneath the surface there is another even more far-
reaching conflict which is not between Jesus and the Pharisees
but between two competing concepts of religion. The
Pharisees come in for a great deal of criticism in the gospels,
not least in Matthew's gospel, and the record needs to be put
straight. They were not necessarily 'pharisaic' in the way in
which we use that pejorative term; they were genuine believers in God, who were concerned for the spiritual renewal
of their people, and enjoyed a huge reputation for piety of life
and uprightness of conduct. They were opposed, for example,
to the use of violence against their Roman masters; they
preferred rather to wait for God to act in his own good time.
There were honourable men among them like Joseph of
Arimathea, looking eagerly for the Kingdom and diligent in
prayer for it. It was their very proximity to the ideals which
our Lord himself held dear that made the confrontation
between them particularly painful.

Jesus would no doubt dearly have loved to have had them
on his side. But the truth must prevail. The truth was that
salvation in Jesus's view was not to be had this way. Religion
was not a matter of achievement, however impressive, but of

dependence. Salvation was never going to be earned; it could only be received. Will power, such as the Law required, was not the royal road to the renewal of Israel or to the Kingdom of God. That is why presumably Jesus refused to be deterred from his practice of meeting with 'sinners' because it was of the very essence of his mission. It was these sinners who were to be the object of his Father's mercy and the recipients of his Father's salvation. It was the prostitutes and the tax-collectors who were to go into the Kingdom before the Pharisees and the Scribes.

This conflict which marked Jesus's ministry in Galilee has been endemic in the Church ever since, and we have the evidences of it all around us. The respectable still occupy the church pew, the 'sinners' feel uneasy in it. The wise and the clever dominate the government of the Church, and the not-so-wise or the not-so-clever feel out of their element. It is the confident and the successful who receive the accolades; the poor and the incompetent, or the feckless, are ignored. The rich man still sits in his palace, dressed in the fine linen of spiritual know-how and public acclaim, and Lazarus un-tended, unobserved, sits at the gate. But the truth of the matter is, as our Lord suggests, Lazarus is on course for Abraham's bosom, Dives is on course for hell (Luke 16:19 –31). This is a hard saying, who can bear it?

4

THE FAMILY

[Mark 3:13–35]

[13]Jesus went up on a mountainside and called to him those he wanted, and they came to him. [14]He appointed twelve—designating them apostles—that they might be with him and that he might send them out to preach [15]and to have authority to drive out demons. [16]These are the twelve he appointed: Simon (to whom he gave the name Peter); [17]James son of Zebedee and his brother John (to them he gave the name Boanerges, which means Sons of Thunder);[18]Andrew, Philip, Bartholomew, Matthew, Thomas, James son of Alphaeus, Thaddaeus, Simon the Zealot [19]and Judas Iscariot, who betrayed him.

[20]Then Jesus entered a house, and again a crowd gathered, so that he and his disciples were not even able to eat. [21]When his family heard about this, they went to take charge of him, for they said, "He is out of his mind."

[22]And the teachers of the law who came down from Jerusalem said, "He is possessed by Beelzebub! By the prince of demons he is driving out demons."

[23]So Jesus called them and spoke to them in parables: "How can Satan drive out Satan? [24]If a kingdom is divided against itself, that kingdom cannot stand. [25]If a house is divided against itself, that house cannot stand. [26]And if Satan opposes himself and is divided, he cannot stand; his end has come. [27]In fact, no-one can enter a strong man's house and carry off his possessions unless he first ties up the strong man. Then he can rob his house. [28]I tell you the truth, all the sins and blasphemies of men will be forgiven them. [29]But whoever blasphemes against the Holy Spirit will never be forgiven; he is guilty of an eternal sin."

[30]He said this because they were saying, "He has an evil spirit."

[31]Then Jesus' mother and brothers arrived. Standing outside, they sent someone in to call him. [32]A crowd was sitting around him, and

they told him, "Your mother and brothers are outside looking for you."

[33]"Who are my mother and my brothers?" he asked.

[34]Then he looked at those seated in a circle around him and said, "Here are my mother and my brothers! [35]Whoever does God's will is my brother and sister and mother."

The interpretation of this passage depends, to some degree, on a right understanding of the format in which it appears, and that in turn requires some knowledge of the way in which books came to be written in the ancient world. The cheapest and most common form of writing material was the clay tablet which was widely used to record commercial transactions or to leave messages. It was an extremely durable medium of communication, and archaeologists have cause to be grateful for the massive supplies of clay tablets which have been turned up accidentally or otherwise in the course of history. But they present problems for any filing system, and they break easily.

A more convenient form of writing material called papyrus was therefore developed, composed of strips of reed which for the sake of convenience could easily be rolled and stored. There are climatic conditions under which such papyrus rolls will last for many centuries, as the discovery of the Dead Sea scrolls (1947–60) illustrates. But for the most part papyrus has a short life, and this is one of the reasons why none of the original manuscripts of the Bible remains. What we have in our Bibles are copies of copies, faithfully transcribed down the years, surviving till our own day, as far as we can tell, in a form very close to the original.

The third form of writing material was the parchment, which was made of animal skin and, being thus more expensive, was reserved for documents of unusual value or books which were in constant use. That is why when Paul asked Timothy to bring his books next time he came (2 Tim. 4:13), he asked especially for 'the parchments', which presumably meant some part either of the Greek or Hebrew Scriptures, which were habitually preserved in this form.

Mark's Gospel

When Mark wrote his gospel he did not presume to think that he was writing Holy Scripture on parchment designed for our edification two thousand years later. Rather, he was writing a brief account of events as he saw them, or heard about them, possibly at the request of the church to which he belonged. It was more like an occasional paper than a book. The scroll he would have used would almost certainly have been laid out in columns (see Jer. 36:23 RSV), thus enabling it to be read in public without having to stretch the roll to its fullest extent.

We know little about the editorial conventions of the day, but we do know that the gospel would not have been divided into chapters and verses, which are a much later device to provide ease of reference. Punctuation was much less complex than it is nowadays, and there was no certain way of telling where reported speech begins and ends. Given the lack of such editorial aids the ancient author had to use other devices to make his point in the actual text.

So St Matthew's gospel is often considered to be divided into five books corresponding to the five books of Moses, marked in his case by a recurring single phrase which would alert the reader to the fact that a new section was beginning. Mark, too, has his devices, and one of the more interesting ones is the practice of 'intercalation'. You will see the method at work here where he begins to tell the story of how Jesus's family were reacting to him, then breaks the narrative to include the story of an encounter with the teachers of the Law who came down from Jerusalem.

The method may be observed at work again at Mark 5:21–36 and Mark 6:13–30. It can be used just for dramatic effect. It has been used by authors for that purpose down the ages. It keeps the audience in suspense while they wait for the dénouement of the story. But it may also be used to associate two distinct events with each other. In Mark 6, for instance, it is used to make the point that the death, the execution and burial of John the Baptist was closely associated with the expansion of the mission of Jesus and his disciples.

In the passage now under consideration it is meant to indicate that at this moment of time the opposition of the teachers from Jerusalem to Jesus's ministry and the opposition of his family proceed alike from the same cause – a gross misunderstanding of him and culpable resistance to God's will. John records that 'even his own brothers did not believe in him' (John 7:5) and elsewhere Mark records Jesus's sorrowful reaction to this unbelief in the words: 'Only in his home town, among his relatives and in his own house is a prophet without honour' (Mark 6:4). The original format, therefore, of this passage is highly significant for its understanding.

Jesus's Family

It is a singular feature of Mark's presentation of the life of Jesus that he records nothing of his birth, upbringing and family connections. He records that Jesus came from Nazareth to the River Jordan to be baptised, but there are no infancy narratives and no allusion to the virgin birth. The family appear on the scene in this passage without any previous reference to them.

For Mark it almost seems as if Jesus was 'without father or mother, without genealogy, without beginning of days or end of life', words which the writer of Hebrews applied to Melchizedek, King of Salem, in the time of Abraham (Heb. 7:3). And when the family do appear, they appear deliberately aligned by the author with the opposition of the official teachers of Israel. They come under the same condemnation. So, why did they come? It has to be remembered that they lived at Nazareth, twenty miles away, and Jesus was based at Capernaum. It was not, therefore, as if they had walked round the corner from the carpenter's shop to have a word with him. It was a concerted act arising out of the conviction of the family that Jesus was 'out of his mind' and a desire to get him again into their own hands.

Their action was perfectly understandable. It was disturbing enough for a member of the family to become associated with a renewal movement in Israel and to be baptised by John the Baptist, especially as it meant leaving home and seemingly cutting himself off from the family. It was even more disturbing to hear of his sudden prominence in and around the towns and villages of Galilee. But it was even worse when it became obvious that his actions were attracting the attention of the leaders of the nation in Jerusalem itself.

Jesus's family were, we must presume, humble members of the synagogue, and would not have been prepared for this kind of publicity. In our day it would have meant callers on the telephone, camera crews at the door, and all the hullabaloo of sudden fame. And they would not have been reassured when they came to see for themselves what was going on – the excited crowds, the miracles of healing, the casting out of demons. These were signs, in their view, reserved for the end of the age and the coming of the Messiah and the restoration of the Kingdom to Israel; they did not associate such events with a member of their ordinary family, who a few months before had been working in the carpenter's shop and writing out the bills, and collecting the money. Moreover, they would not be unaware that the leader of a similar movement in Israel had already paid the price of his temerity, had been arrested, imprisoned in Herod's fortress at Machaerus, and was now dead and buried.

The scene is not unlike the story of the marriage in Cana recounted in John's gospel (2:1–11), where Mary interceded with her son to ease a situation in which the host was running short of wine. She is rewarded with a seemingly harsh utterance, extremely difficult to translate into English, but meaning something like 'What do you and I have in common?' (John 2:4). Jesus was no doubt an affectionate son, but kinship was not allowed to deflect him from the task which his Father had given him to do. He must be about his Father's business (Luke 2:49). No one, therefore, whether it be the Scribes from Jerusalem or his family from Nazareth, could be permitted to stand in his way. This is the only reference to Mary in Mark's gospel, and in common with the other synoptists he does not include her among the women who were present at Calvary.

History is silent about other members of the family, with the striking exception of James, who, by processes no longer known to us, became head of the Church in Jerusalem, and Jude his brother who succeeded him. So, whatever the motives which impelled the family to seek out Jesus, it is clear that one at least came to perceive the true nature of Jesus's calling and ultimately to respond to him in faith.

Reactions in the Church

The reader will hardly be surprised to hear that the Church at large has found it difficult down the ages to come to terms with this passage in the gospel – and for varying reasons. The first is that commentators have been puzzled by the fact that Mary should ever think that her son was 'out of his mind'. Had she not heard the angel's voice? Did she not believe that he would be great, and would be called the Son of the Most High, that he would be given the throne of his father David, and would reign over the house of Jacob for ever (Luke 1:32–3)? How could such a transcending vision be erased by the mere passage of time?

Mark himself might have been able to say that he had known what it was to have a clear call, be a missionary of the gospel – and then just to go back home dispirited and afraid. But Mark does not often offer any psychological explanation for the events which he records – nor, indeed, is he under any obligation to do so. He is not haunted by, or even may not be aware of, the dramatic stories of Matthew and Luke about the birth in Bethlehem, the song of the angels, and the coming of the shepherds and the wise men. If we were relying on Mark's narrative alone there would be no 'Christmas' as we normally understand it.

The second problem for the Church has been the reference to Jesus's brothers. Growing reverence for Mary led, by the end of the fourth century, to a tradition of her 'perpetual virginity', that is to say that she had no further children after Jesus. The appearance of 'the brothers' in this passage appears to challenge that tradition, and commentators have gone to some lengths to offer explanations which avoid this seeming conflict between tradition and Scripture. It has been suggested, for example, that the word can mean just relatives, or that they were sons of Joseph by a former wife.

It is this tradition which has presumably influenced the art of the nativity. Have you ever seen a young Joseph in a stained-glass window, or on a Christmas card? So, Bede, writing in the eighth century, says 'the brothers of the Lord must not be thought to be the sons of the ever-virgin Mary, or the sons of Joseph by a former marriage, as some think, but rather they must be understood to be his relations.' This is one obvious example of the way in which doctrinal development can have a profound influence on the way in which Scripture is interpreted. The plain meaning of the text is that they were brothers.

For Mark, the true understanding of Jesus does not depend on the circumstances of his birth or a unique relationship with his mother: rather, it follows from the plain, unadorned record of his life and ministry from about the age of 30 onwards. For Mark, as we shall discover in the course of this study, it was Jesus's 'distance' from humanity which marked everything that he said or did. He refused to conform to the religious fashions of the day; he was not susceptible to the pressures of society or of his family. He enjoyed a special relationship with his heavenly Father which was not shared by anyone else. He had a view of his mission which even his closest associates did not understand. He was alone, bearing the burdens of a calling which transcends our understanding and defies our imitation. In the mountain range of prophets and seers, of kings and wise men, Jesus towers above them all in lonely and awesome splendour. This is the mystery of his being, as Mark sees it, and he resolutely confines himself to this theme, eschewing interesting additions, offering no explanations, drawing no conclusions. His is, to use a technical term, a 'kerygmatic' story: it is the story of what Jesus did and said and what happened to him.

Mark may have owed much to Peter's way of telling that story, but the gospel is his own, and for that very reason it is quite distinct from anything that was written by Paul,

Matthew, Luke or John. To him the negative encounter with the family is part of his understanding of the true nature of Christ – a member of the human family but more, a member of the Jewish race but more, a vehicle of God's Word but more, the anointed Saviour of Israel, but more . . .

A Pronouncement Story

The call of Levi was a 'conflict story'. The encounter with Jesus's family is often called a 'pronouncement story'. This is part of the vocabulary of 'Form Criticism' which seeks to understand the gospel as the product of a long process of telling and retelling the story in the early Church. It has been a valuable tool, but is open to the criticism that such a process, common in all ancient literature, has had little time to operate in the case of the gospels.

Mark is writing within forty years of the events recorded in his gospel, forty years indeed of hectic activity by the Church and devoted proclamation of the truth about Jesus, but scarcely time for the development of a sophisticated literary tradition. However, this is certainly a 'pronouncement story', setting the scene, describing the action, then enunciating a principle which is to be of far-reaching importance in the life of the Church – 'whoever does God's will is my brother and sister and mother' (v. 35).

In that saying he abolishes any claims based on consanguinity, or superior learning or membership of a prestigious group. His family and his opponents will have to learn the lesson that the only qualification for God's favour is doing God's will. We would have been spared many unnecessary troubles if the principle had always been observed in the Church.

In Jesus's day many groups within Israel vied for supremacy and privilege on the basis of a special allegiance, e.g. Pharisees, Sadducees, Herodians, Zealots, Essenes, followers of John the Baptist. They all clamoured for the ear of the public. They vied with each other for a special position in God's providence. But the message is clear. You do not earn

God's favour by being a Jew or a Christian, by being a Baptist or an Anglican or a Roman Catholic, by being a monk or a nun, by being a bishop or a priest. God's favour cannot be earned. It is the gift of God, to those, and those alone, who do his will. According to St John it was the ultimate claim made for Jesus himself – "'I am come down from heaven, not to do mine own will but the will of him that sent me'" (John 6:38, RV).

5

THE DEMON-POSSESSED MAN

[Mark 4:35–5:20]

³⁵That day when evening came, he said to his disciples, "Let us go over to the other side." ³⁶Leaving the crowd behind, they took him along, just as he was, in the boat. There were also other boats with him. ³⁷A furious squall came up, and the waves broke over the boat, so that it was nearly swamped. ³⁸Jesus was in the stern, sleeping on a cushion. The disciples woke him and said to him, "Teacher, don't you care if we drown?"

³⁹He got up, rebuked the wind and said to the waves, "Quiet! Be still!" Then the wind died down and it was completely calm.

⁴⁰He said to his disciples, "Why are you so afraid? Do you still have no faith?"

⁴¹They were terrified and asked each other, "Who is this? Even the wind and the waves obey him!"

5 They went across the lake to the region of the Gerasenes. ²When Jesus got out of the boat, a man with an evil spirit came from the tombs to meet him. ³This man lived in the tombs, and no-one could bind him any more, not even with a chain. ⁴For he had often been chained hand and foot, but he tore the chains apart and broke the irons on his feet. No-one was strong enough to subdue him. ⁵Night and day among the tombs and in the hills he would cry out and cut himself with stones.

⁶When he saw Jesus from a distance, he ran and fell on his knees in front of him. ⁷He shouted at the top of his voice, "What do you want with me, Jesus, Son of the Most High God? Swear to God that you won't torture me!" ⁸For Jesus had said to him, "Come out of this man, you evil spirit!"

⁹Then Jesus asked him, "What is your name?"

"My name is Legion," he replied, "for we are many." ¹⁰And he begged Jesus again and again not to send them out of the area.

¹¹A large herd of pigs was feeding on the nearby hillside. ¹²The

demons begged Jesus, "Send us among the pigs; allow us to go into them." [13]He gave them permission, and the evil spirits came out and went into the pigs. The herd, about two thousand in number, rushed down the steep bank into the lake and were drowned.

[14]Those tending the pigs ran off and reported this in the town and countryside, and the people went out to see what had happened. [15]When they came to Jesus, they saw the man who had been possessed by the legion of demons, sitting there, dressed and in his right mind; and they were afraid. [16]Those who had seen it told the people what had happened to the demon-possessed man—and told about the pigs as well. [17]Then the people began to plead with Jesus to leave their region.

[18]As Jesus was getting into the boat, the man who had been demon-possessed begged to go with him. [19]Jesus did not let him, but said, "Go home to your family and tell them how much the Lord has done for you, and how he has had mercy on you." [20]So the man went away and began to tell in the Decapolis how much Jesus had done for him. And all the people were amazed.

If we were approaching the gospel as a biography, we might well ask three questions about the passage we now consider. Where did Jesus actually go when he set off across the lake? Why did he go? When did he come back? We have had cause to observe before that notes of time and place in the gospels are vague. This is hardly surprising. I can remember vividly certain events from the distant past – the place, the conversation, the kind of room and the view out of the window. But thirty or forty years later I should not have the slightest idea where the incident fitted in, or what were the circumstances which led to it. Mark, relying as we presume on Peter's memory of the events, and possibly without any knowledge of the area, can do little more than record what he hears and has himself to supply the links between the incidents.

So we have phrases like 'on another occasion', or 'when he was alone', or 'when evening came', or just 'then', or 'immediately'. So we shall have to disabuse ourselves of any idea that an exact itinerary or chronology can be created out of the gospels. The narratives may well have an inner coherence, but that coherence may be based on considerations other than those of time and place. Nevertheless, the three questions are of some importance in assessing the significance of the healing of the demon-possessed man.

Where did Jesus go?

On what part of the coast did Jesus arrive after their stormy crossing? The footnote to this passage in the NIV records that some manuscripts read 'region of the Gadarenes', other manuscripts read 'Gergesenes'. So we have three possibilities within the Marcan text alone. The transmission of any ancient manuscript is subject to the usual accidents: a reference may be changed by a simple copying mistake, or it may be changed deliberately to correct what in the scribe's view is an obvious error. Either of these principles may be at work in this passage. The only thing that can be said confidently is that Jesus arrived with his disciples on the opposite side of the lake from Capernaum, that is to say on the eastern shore.

Matthew, writing on the basis of Mark, opts for 'Gadarenes', Luke opts for 'Gerasenes'. There are problems, however, about both these sites. Gadara, one of the towns of the Decapolis, is more than ten miles from the shore of the lake, and Gerasa is even further. This leaves 'Gergesenes' as the more likely reading, one which is supported by many scholars including Origen, one of the earliest of them. He observed from his personal knowledge of the Holy Land that Gergesa (later known as Khersa) was on a slope down which the swine could run into the sea, and it was much nearer Capernaum than either of the other two sites. If Gergesa is the right reading it is easy to see how it came to be altered. Gadara and Gerasa were large towns and well known in the ancient world, Gergesa was a place of little importance, and the scribe may well have decided that one of the other towns was meant.

Decapolis

The area known as Decapolis (see map) was not one of the territories occupied by the tribes of Israel when they entered Canaan. It became part of the empire of David and later of Solomon. It was incorporated in the Greek empire after the conquests of Alexander in the fourth century and was subsequently ruled by the Seleucid kings until it was subjugated by the Jewish king John Hircanus, who reigned from 134–104 BC. When Pompey invaded Palestine in 64–63 BC, he liberated the ten cities of the Decapolis. They were annexed to the Roman province of Syria and enjoyed a high degree of municipal freedom. It follows that Decapolis by the time of Jesus was essentially a Greek area dominated by Greek customs, Greek buildings and Greek culture, but there would have remained at least an element of the old Jewish population which would no doubt have clung to its own traditions, but could hardly have been immune to the cultural and religious pressures of the society in which they found themselves. They may even have kept pigs.

Why did Jesus go?

This brings us to the second question. Why did Jesus cross the lake at all, whether it was to Gergesa, Gerasa or Gadara? It is suggested elsewhere in the gospel that Jesus often used the boat as a 'floating pulpit' from which to address the people on the shore, or fishermen in other boats nearby. But he used it also to escape from the attentions of the crowd. The 'crowd' everywhere forms the background of the gospel – entranced by his teaching, or hostile and unbelieving, eager to make use of the healing power which Jesus so manifestly possessed, and yet often unconvinced by the exercise of this power, sometimes responding to him as the leader of a new spiritual renewal in Israel, at other times seeing in him the possibility of a new political ruler and the overthrow of Rome. So prominent is this noisy, chaotic crowd in the life of Jesus, that Mark sometimes takes note of it when on rare occasions Jesus manages to be on his own with his disciples. So the departure across the lake on the evening of that day when he had been teaching the people may have been no more than an escape from the crowd who otherwise thrust themselves upon him and gave him no liberty of action. There was nowhere else to go but across the lake where he could not be followed except by a long overland route.

If that is so, then the incidents which followed were entirely unpremeditated and accidental. But it is possible that we have here another Marcan example of Jesus's mission to the Gentiles on a par with his later visit to the region of Tyre and Sidon (Mark 7:24–30). In this case the demon-possessed man would have been a Gentile not a Jew, and the proclamation of the good news in Decapolis would have been seen by Mark's readers as the origin of the Christian mission in that area, maybe even the founding of a Christian congregation there.

Tradition has it that after the fall of Jerusalem some Christians fled to Pella, which is one of the cities of the Decapolis near enough to Judea to be easily accessible to it. So it is of some consequence whether it was to Gadara, Gerasa or Gergesa that Jesus went. Gergesa was in the territory of Philip the tetrarch, where the population would have been predominantly Jewish rather than Gentile.

Mark seldom offers any psychological explanation for Jesus's actions, and does not indulge in speculation about Jesus's inner life. This could hardly be otherwise, because he had no access to information about it, and the search for 'the Jesus of history' had not begun. To his informants and to his readers the only thing that mattered was that Jesus had lived, taught, died and risen from the dead – and would come again. In that scenario there was no space for the kind of enquiry which has fascinated so many of later generations. They knew him 'after the spirit', they welcomed his presence at the assemblies and were content to worship him as Lord of heaven and earth. But even if the search for the inner life of Jesus can yield no certain results, yet we in our generation can hardly be indifferent to it, and the author of the fourth gospel certainly made a start in his version of the events.

We must allow, therefore, for a third possible answer to the question – why did Jesus cross the lake that evening? If it was not entirely accidental and it was not an early 'Gentile mission', what was it? I have commented already on the sense of 'distance' between Jesus and even those who were closest to him. He had his own hopes, fears, anxieties, without which he would not have been human at all. But he was sustained in them, as St John makes clear, by the experience of an unparalleled intimacy with his Father in heaven. He was not at the mercy of the crowd; he did not always respond to his disciples' suggestions. He was not unaffected by the circumstances under which he lived, but he was not dominated by them. He loved his disciples, but his greatest love was for the Father whom he experienced in his own times of prayer and quiet. He attended to the crowds, but he waited on God.

So it could be that his decision to cross the lake that evening did not arise from his desire to escape the crowd, or to engage in an exemplary 'mission to the Gentiles', but from his own habit of waiting on God. John records two instances in his gospel which show Jesus in the same attitude of 'waiting'. In John 7 his brothers press him to go to Jerusalem for the Feast of the Tabernacles in order, as they said, that 'your disciples may see the miracles you do' (John 7:3). He demurred and remained in Galilee, but when his brothers had gone, with whom he presumably would have travelled, he decided to go on his own 'in secret'. The story represents once again the growing distance between his family and himself, but it also shows that he was uncertain about how to act, and waited for his Father's guidance.

The same hesitation seems to attach to the story of Lazarus. When he heard that he was sick he stayed for two days in the place where he was (John 11:6). Then he said to his disciples, 'Let us go back to Judaea' (v. 7). His disciples, not unnaturally, reacted against the suggestion because, as they said, they would be in danger of stoning if they went. Nevertheless Jesus went, and John, I suppose, at this stage in the gospel, is inviting us to see that this was to be a crucial decision leading ultimately to Jesus's arrest and execution. Once again he was waiting upon God for the decisive voice.

If we find this strange to our experience, it shows how

unfamiliar we have become with what was to the old Israel
and to the new an essential ingredient of their faith. Samuel
anointed Saul as king (by any standards a significant development in the life of Israel) for no better reason than that he was
commanded of God to do so. In a time of famine Elijah took
himself off to Zarephath for no better reason than that God
had commanded him to do so. Philip terminated a successful
mission in Samaria to go down to the desert – at the word of
God – and indirectly became the founder of the church in
Ethiopia. Ananias, an inconspicuous member of the church in
Damascus, was commanded – much to his dismay – to visit
Saul in the Street called Straight, and in so doing made
possible the mission to the Gentiles. Jesus observed the same
principle in his own life and proved himself 'an Israelite
indeed'. The fruit of his obedience was a mighty demonstration of power in the stilling of the storm, and an equally
mighty demonstration of power in the healing of the possessed man – which led itself to the proclamation of good news in
the Greek cities of the Decapolis.

The third question we have to answer is – when did Jesus
come back? It can briefly be answered. We do not know,
neither are we in a position at this distance away to reconstruct these incidents in any convincing order. They are linked
not by time or place but by subject. The stilling of the storm
and the healing of the demon-possessed man are both concerned with 'demons', and the exact details of time and place
are irrelevant to them both.

The Demons

The difficulties of time and place in the gospel will seem very
minor to most readers in comparison with the difficulties
raised by 'demons'. Here we enter a world which was very
familiar to Jesus and his contemporaries, but, apart from the
occasional report in the press on the subject, is largely
unfamiliar to most of us. There is no point in trying to explain
the problem away by pretending that it is simply a matter of
words. The statistics of the New Testament do not permit any

evasion of the issue. The word for 'being possessed' occurs thirteen times, the word for 'demon' sixty times, the word for 'the unclean spirit' (which means much the same) twenty-one times.

The world in which Jesus lived was haunted by demons. They lay in wait for unsuspecting travellers. They could get inside you if you slept with your mouth open at night. They could get into your body if you were not very careful on the food you ate. They created chaos in the life of individuals and in the life of society. They were taken very seriously by the gospel writers and by the early Church. The demon-possessed man spoke of his demons as 'legion' – and the normal Roman legion numbered five thousand men. Any man who was mad or out of his mind was said to have a demon. This was alleged of John the Baptist (Matt. 11:18), and of Jesus himself (John 10:20).

The mythology of the demons' origin varied. In the Greek mind they were regarded as minor deities. In the Hebrew mind they were regarded as the servants of Satan, great adversary of God and man, who marshalled his forces against the Kingdom of God. So, therefore, when Jesus spoke as he often did of 'the Kingdom of God', he reflected, by implication at least, the existence of another kingdom (of Satan) opposed to it. He encountered the opposition of Satan in his own temptations at the beginning of his ministry, and he was to encounter Satan's subjects repeatedly thereafter. The story of the encounter with the demon-possessed man was simply one of many.

It was believed that the home base of the 'demons' was in the 'abyss', a word which is used by Luke in the parallel passage (Luke 8:31). It was from the abyss that the marauding demons arose, to perpetrate their evils upon earth, and it was to the abyss that the Gergesene demons were consigned by the pigs which ran down the slope into the sea. The connection with the preceding story of the stilling of the storm must by now be obvious. When Jesus spoke to the demons he used a word 'quiet, be still', which in the language of sacred Scripture sounds restrained and dignified, but is actually a word which is used in the contemporary world for telling a dog or a child to 'shut up'. He was rebuking the demons of the abyss who had stirred up the storm which threatened to engulf them all.

Did Jesus believe in demons? It is possible to hedge the question and to say that he used the language he did and performed the actions he did because he had to accommodate himself to the beliefs of those to whom he ministered. But readers of the gospel who desire to understand it must come to terms with the fact that Jesus was a Jew of the first century, his mind formed not only by the sacred Scriptures of his people but by their habits of thought and their assumptions. No man can be immune to the world view of his time. He was a first-century not a twentieth-century or a fifteenth-century man. The belief in demons was a world view common to all ancient civilisations under whatever guises demons appeared to them.

So the answer must be 'yes', he did believe in demons. He acted out that belief in the stilling of the storm and the healing of the demon-possessed man, and elsewhere in his references to Satan and to the kingdom of Satan in this world. That is why the practice of exorcism features so strongly in the gospels, and why it has continued in the life of the Church down to our own time.

When he uttered the words recorded by St John at his crucifixion – 'It is finished' (John 19:30) it was not understood by John to be a sigh of relief that the agony was over, but a sign of triumph that the essential conflict between God and the devil had been won. From beginning to end, Jesus's ministry was conducted in the atmosphere of that conflict of which the healing of the sick, exorcisms and the battle with unbelief were all part. When he rebuked Peter with the words 'Get behind me, Satan!' (Mark 8:33), he meant exactly what he said. At that moment Peter, for all his seeming solicitude, was in the grip of the evil one who opposed God's Kingdom on earth. The gospel narratives are incomprehensible if this world view is disregarded.

Can we believe in Demons?

If Jesus believed in demons, do we have to believe in them? If he saw the Kingdom of God arrayed against Satan, do we have to believe it? Let us allow at once that we do not altogether share the world view of two thousand years ago; we do not see the charming countryside of North Oxfordshire as the abode of demons into which we stray when we leave behind the securities of the city or the village. As children we do not have our mouths firmly closed by our parents to avoid the peril of demon possession; we do not scrutinise our food for the evidence of their presence.

We are, however, vividly aware of irrational forces at work in society and in ourselves, such as phobias, complexes, paranoias, obsessions, irresistible urges. We assault old people for no obvious reason. We decapitate young children and bury them without motive. We fling ourselves upon rivals in the football stand for no better reason than that they wear a different-coloured scarf. We threaten each other with hydrogen bombs and lethal lasers, knowing all the time that to use these weapons would be to terminate our existence on earth. The Roman legion is hardly numerous enough to list our ills.

Even if we disown the language of the ancient Hebrews or the ancient Greeks, we have to devise a language of our own to describe not dissimilar phenomena. There is, it seems, a kingdom of evil against a kingdom of righteousness, and it matters a great deal to which kingdom we belong. The demon-possessed man at Gergesa knew to which kingdom he had belonged, and took to his Gentile neighbours in Decapolis good news – there was someone about on the other side of the lake who could cast the demons out.

The difficulties of determining the exact text and following Jesus's journeys on a map ought not to blind us to the quite extraordinary vividness which attaches to this section of the gospel. The details of the narrative are of a kind that could hardly be invented even by a supreme literary artist. They bear the mark of well-remembered personal testimony. If Peter was Mark's informant, he may be forgiven for a certain vagueness of memory regarding time and place, but his account itself suggests the excitement of someone on whose mind a new truth was dawning – 'Who is this, that even the wind and the waves obey him?'

The same question resounds throughout the narrative – 'Who is this who conquers the demons; who is this who cures the incurable and raises the dead?' So in the surrounding unbelief and rejection which manifested itself at this stage in Jesus's ministry, there is one man at least in whose mind is being prepared the great affirmation which he is later to make and which has become the foundation-stone of the Christian Church, 'You are the Christ.' We shall see later the astounding truth which this represents. We only observe for the moment the origins of that faith in his earlier exposure to the unparalleled works of God made visible in the life of his servant, Jesus.

6

JAIRUS, RULER OF THE SYNAGOGUE

[Mark 5:21–43]

[21] When Jesus had again crossed over by boat to the other side of the lake, a large crowd gathered round him while he was by the lake. [22] Then one of the synagogue rulers, named Jairus, came there. Seeing Jesus, he fell at his feet [23] and pleaded earnestly with him, "My little daughter is dying. Please come and put your hands on her so that she will be healed and live." [24] So Jesus went with him.

A large crowd followed and pressed around him. [25] And a woman was there who had been subject to bleeding for twelve years. [26] She had suffered a great deal under the care of many doctors and had spent all she had, yet instead of getting better she grew worse. [27] When she heard about Jesus, she came up behind him in the crowd and touched his cloak, [28] because she thought, "If I just touch his clothes, I will be healed." [29] Immediately her bleeding stopped and she felt in her body that she was freed from her suffering.

[30] At once Jesus realised that power had gone out from him. He turned around in the crowd and asked, "Who touched my clothes?"

[31] "You see the people crowding against you," his disciples answered, "and yet you can ask, 'Who touched me?'"

[32] But Jesus kept looking around to see who had done it. [33] Then the woman, knowing what had happened to her, came and fell at his feet and, trembling with fear, told him the whole truth. [34] He said to her, "Daughter, your faith has healed you. Go in peace and be freed from your suffering."

[35] While Jesus was still speaking, some men came from the house of Jairus, the synagogue ruler. "Your daughter is dead," they said. "Why bother the teacher any more?"

[36] Ignoring what they said, Jesus told the synagogue ruler, "Don't be afraid; just believe."

[37] He did not let anyone follow him except Peter, James and John the

brother of James. [38]When they came to the home of the synagogue ruler, Jesus saw a commotion, with people crying and wailing loudly. [39]He went in and said to them, "Why all this commotion and wailing? The child is not dead but asleep." [40]But they laughed at him.

After he put them all out, he took the child's father and mother and the disciples who were with him, and went in where the child was. [41]He took her by the hand and said to her, "*Talitha koum!*" (which means, "Little girl, I say to you, get up!"). [42]Immediately the girl stood up and walked around (she was twelve years old). At this they were completely astonished. [43]He gave strict orders not to let anyone know about this, and told them to give her something to eat.

Luke permits himself an elegant little introduction to this section – 'Now when Jesus returned [from Gergesa] a crowd welcomed him, for they were all expecting him' (Luke 8:40). Mark by contrast does not attempt any literary link, and simply records that Jesus is once more engulfed in the crowds from which he had so briefly escaped the previous day.

The stilling of the storm and the casting out of the demons had an obvious connection with each other – both were examples of Jesus's power over the forces of Satan. There is no such obvious connection in the passage we are now considering. The language is more marked than usual by Semitisms, that is to say, written in Greek but reflecting Semitic constructions and, indeed, including an Aramaic phrase at the end. This suggests a Palestinian source for the narrative, and it would be reasonable to suppose that Mark owed it to his chief informant, Peter himself.

It is vivid and circumstantial, carrying with it still the sense of excitement which Jesus's return to Galilee generated among the people. There does not have to be any thematic connection between the two events recorded in this passage. It could be that they just happened this way. Nevertheless, the relationship between them is instructive, insofar as it emphasises certain contrasts.

Jairus is the first to appear on the scene. We know his name, and we know that he was an important person in the life of the community. The woman on the other hand has no name, and certainly no claim on the time and attention of Jesus. One early historian, Eusebius, suggests that she came from Paneas, otherwise known as Caesarea Philippi, or Banias, now well established on the modern tourist route. In the woman's case, healing resulted from an emission of power from Jesus before he becomes aware of it, whereas Jairus's daughter is healed by a deliberate act. The healing of the woman takes place in the midst of a dense crowd, whereas in the healing of Jairus's daughter the crowd is deliberately kept at bay and the miracle is known only to Jesus, three disciples and Jairus's household.

While we are dealing with contrasts it would be sensible to mention another possible one. The ruler of the synagogue stands for an ancient and prestigious religion whereas, if Eusebius is right, the woman came from an area marked more by an enthusiasm for heathen rites than for devotion to the God of Israel. It is said by Eusebius that in his day a house in Banias was known to visitors to the Holy Land, near which had been raised a bronze figure of a woman kneeling, stretching out her hands for help. Opposite her stood the statue of a male figure which, it is said, bore the likeness of Jesus. So she had a stone memorial to her faith. Jairus has no such memorial. But faith is the medium of healing in both cases, e.g. 'your faith has healed you' (v. 34), 'Don't be afraid; just believe' (v. 36).

The Woman

If the woman lived at Banias she had come a long way seeking for health, nearly thirty miles – without benefit of train or car or even a horse – her determination no doubt fuelled by the nature of her illness. A woman with her complaint today could be cured by a relatively common operation which would have set her on the path to health. She, on the other hand, suffered with it for twelve years 'under the care of many doctors and had spent all she had, yet instead of getting better she grew worse' (v. 26). When you compare this version with that of St Luke you will notice that Luke, as a physician himself, qualifies this seeming attack on his profession and observes only that 'no-one could heal her' (Luke 8:43).

But in addition to not having access to medical techniques which are familiar to us, she suffered from a further disability in that her particular illness was regarded by Jewish Law as a ritual uncleanness which disqualified the sufferer from normal social intercourse. So she was taking refuge in the anonymity of the crowd when she stole up behind Jesus and touched his cloak.

It may be of interest to observe that both Matthew and Luke enlarge the record slightly by saying that she touched 'the edge of his cloak'. The word translated 'edge' could refer to the tassels at the four corners of an outer garment worn by an accredited teacher of the Law. This little point was presumably thought to be of importance by Matthew and Luke, because it heightened the contrast between Jesus the Jewish teacher and the social outcast.

The woman's action was not, in one sense, remarkable, because it was generally believed in the ancient world that the powers of healing resided in the clothing, or even in the shadow, of a holy man (cf. Acts 5:15; 19:12). What was remarkable was that Jesus himself should have been aware that power had gone out from him – which provoked the rather brusque retort by the disciples.

We can understand their bewilderment. With people pressing all around him, like an Indian crowd in a bazaar, how could he possibly ask who touched him? But he was aware that something had happened, and aware, too, that the woman's action was not just the product of a heathenish superstition but of a burgeoning, if uninformed, faith. It was indeed a remarkable event, not only for the woman but for Jesus. It may have been to him a signal discovery about his own powers and about his own role. But, significant though it was for the two people most closely involved, it must have seemed both to Jairus and to Jesus's disciples an unwonted and troublesome interruption of the business they had in hand – which was to attend to the desperate need of a very important person, the ruler of the synagogue.

The Synagogue

To appreciate the 'inwardness' of the story it is necessary to know something of the place of the synagogue in the life of Israel. Oddly enough, for an institution so prominent at the time of Jesus and so familiar down to our own day, we know singularly little about its origin. Synagogues play a highly significant part in the writings of the New Testament. There are eight references to them in Mark, nine in Matthew, fifteen in Luke, two in John and twenty in Acts. It is said, though perhaps with pious exaggeration, that there were between three and four hundred synagogues in Jerusalem alone, and they would have been an integral part of Jewish life and religion in Galilee. It used to be assumed that the synagogue system derived from the dispersion of the Jews after the fall of Jerusalem in 586 – a natural assumption given the fact that, deprived of access to the Temple, Jews needed some alternative centre for their religion.

But it could be that the origins of the synagogue go back behind Ezra and that it co-existed with the Temple, offering not an alternative but a parallel institution in the life of the Jewish community. This is more than of just antiquarian interest; it throws some light on the development of Hebrew religion in the centuries preceding the birth of Christ. It is significant that Ezra read the Law at a series of great public assemblies (Neh. 8). The Law increasingly became a public property which was heard, taught, discussed Sabbath by Sabbath – not in the restored Temple but in assemblies large and small in the towns and villages of Judah and Galilee. Such an assembly would have been called a 'synagogue', that is the 'gathering together'.

By contrast with the Temple, which was under the control of a priestly caste, the synagogue was essentially a lay organ- isation, served indeed by scholars and teachers of the Law, but run by prominent people in the community with no necessary claims to priestly descent or to academic expertise. The synagogue, moreover, and especially so in Greek towns where Jews lived, was more than a religious centre; it was the centre of the total community life. Thus the building served as a primary school and a court of local government. It served as a Town Hall and as a lodging-place for travellers. Punishment for offences against Jewish Law was executed in it (Mark 13:9). Lay men and lay women played a prominent part in its life, and it was indeed a high honour to be appointed 'Ruler of the Synagogue'. It is not surprising, therefore, that the name given to the modern Israeli parliament is derived from one of the words for synagogue – Knesset.

Jairus played a very important role not just in his synagogue but in the minds of the evangelists. As in the case of Nicodemus, a ruler of the Jews in Jerusalem, it was striking that the ruler of the synagogue should throw his dignity to the winds and kneel at the feet (Matt. 9:18) of this unofficial teacher and healer from Nazareth. It was a matter of life and death for him, but it was also a matter of great importance to the evangelists, living as they did in a world in which there developed a fierce rivalry between the Christian church and the Jewish synagogue.

Occasionally fierce persecution broke out against the Christians, and men like Paul were punished in the synagogues for their adherence to the Christian cause (see Acts 18). Such a story as this read at one of those early Christian assemblies would have provoked a strong reaction in the minds of those who heard it – to think that a ruler of the synagogue should once come to Jesus for the healing of his daughter, and had not come in vain.

The delay created by the woman from Banias could have been critical – and so it proved to be. Members of Jairus's household arrived with the news that his daughter was dead. There was no need to bother the teacher any more – a remark which perhaps justifies a suggestion made by some commentators that his servants wanted to spare their master the embarrassment of having Jesus come to his home. It is not absolutely clear whether the word translated 'ignoring' means ignoring or overhearing, but in any case Jesus brushed the news aside. 'Don't be afraid; just believe'.

At this point the crowd, highly excited though it was, melted away and at Jesus's command did not accompany him to the ruler of the synagogue's house. He took just three of his disciples and arrived to find the traditional mourning ceremonies already in progress. When he said that the girl was just asleep they laughed at him. It is not clear how exactly Mark understood the story at this point, but Luke leaves the reader in no doubt: 'They laughed at him, knowing that she was dead' (Luke 8:53).

What follows is a stunning exercise of power conducted with the minimum show. When the author of 2 Kings related a somewhat similar miracle, he described how Elisha went in 'and lay upon the child, and put his mouth upon his mouth, and his eyes upon his eyes and his hands upon his hands: and he stretched himself upon the child, and the flesh oi the child waxed warm' (2 Kings 4:34 AV). But in Jesus's case the act is accomplished by the taking of the child's hand and two Aramaic words. There was no groaning of spirit, no agony of prayer, no magic incantations. He spoke and it was done.

The Miracle

Does Mark's narrative require Luke's strong asseveration that the child really was dead and not just, for example, in a coma? The series of events which we have been studying in this section are examples in ascending order of the mighty works of God by the hand of his servant Jesus. It is quite clear to me, though not, it must be said, to all commentators, that Mark sees the raising of Jairus's daughter as the culminating point to this stage of Jesus's ministry. Luke elsewhere records the raising of a young man, the son of the widow of Main (Luke 7:11–17). John records the raising of Lazarus which in his view represents the ultimate challenge of Jesus to the religious authorities in Jerusalem, and did indeed provoke his arrest and execution (John 11:1–50). What is striking about Mark's narrative here is that this stupendous miracle is recorded in such a low key. There were no crowds to view it, there is no statement of astonishment and the Aramaic words used by Jesus are ordinary homely words which might be used by any parent trying to get a child ready for school – 'time to get up'.

The raising of Jairus's daughter raises in an acute form the problem that faces every modern reader of the gospel – did these things really happen? Is it conceivable that Jesus could still a raging sea, deliver a madman from his madness by a word, heal an incurable disease without knowing it, take a dead girl by the hand and lift her up?

The Jews of our Lord's day were not, as we might suppose, credulous people. They had learned, for example, to distinguish between true prophecy and false, between magic and true religion, between a servant of God and a charlatan (see Acts 8:9–25). Even the disciples show themselves from time to time sceptical and unbelieving. But the incidents of which we have been reading are the record which Mark received from the apostles and from Peter in particular. They were as astonished as any twentieth-century man might be at the unprecedented events which unfolded before them, but they believed – on the evidence of their own eyes and ears.

We cannot lightly dismiss this testimony because it is the only testimony we have. We may, indeed, argue and speculate about these events, but we were not there to see them. The fact that huge crowds followed Jesus from place to place is evidence that the disciples were not alone in their impressions of his power and grace. The miracles are not the product of a fevered imagination: they are recorded with the utmost restraint and with vivid, circumstantial detail. I recall these words which that strange genius George Macdonald, a man who had his own share of doubts, said:

> The miracles of Jesus are the ordinary works of his Father wrought small and swift that we might take them in . . . the mission undertaken by the Son was not to show himself as having all power in heaven and earth but to reveal his Father, to show Him to men such as He is that men may know Him and knowing trust Him. (*Unspoken Sermons*, second series)

If, as we believe, God, the creator of the universe and the Lord of all history, is in Christ, then we ought not to be surprised that things happen which transcend what we like to call the normal and defeat our efforts to explain them.

Dominant Themes

Certain themes run through this section which recur throughout the gospel. The first is the seemingly deliberate contrast
between formal religion and real religion. Under normal
circumstances his role as ruler of the synagogue and his assent
to the Law would have been sufficient for Jairus. But when his
world collapses and his daughter is at death's door, it is not to
the synagogue that he turns but to this way-out itinerant
preacher and healer from Nazareth.

The same theme appears in chapter 1 of this gospel. It was
the Sabbath when all good, right-thinking Jews would have
attended the synagogue. But it was when the Sabbath was
over, the sacred books had been put away, the congregation
had dispersed, the verger was locking up the building, that
real things began to happen and the people besieged Jesus's
home for the healing of the sick and the demon-possessed
(Mark 1:32-4).

Another closely-related theme is the palpable contrast
between the enthusiasm of the crowds, many of whom would
have sat very lightly to their religious duties, and the scepti-
cism and downright opposition of those who took their religion seriously. It is no accident that immediately after the
raising of Jairus's daughter Jesus went back to his own
home-town and taught in the synagogue on the Sabbath. The
congregation were amazed, but took offence at him. Jesus,
for his part, was amazed at their lack of faith, and delivered
himself of a poignant judgment on his own people when he
said 'Only in his home town, among his relatives and in his
own house is a prophet without honour' (Mark 6:4).

The third theme is obviously dear to Mark's heart. In
common parlance, faith is set in apposition to unbelief. In
Mark's vocabulary it is more often set over against fear. 'Why
are you so afraid? Do you still have no faith?' (Mark 4:40).
The woman with the issue of blood came trembling with fear
and told him the whole truth. Jesus said to her: 'Daughter,
your faith has healed you. Go in peace' (Mark 5:34). When
the members of Jairus's household came to him with the
grim news that his daughter was dead, Jesus brushed

the news aside and said, 'Don't be afraid; just believe' (Mark 5:36).

Fear, in Jesus's view, challenges any claim to believe in God as our maker and Father. Mark knew about fear – he had deserted Paul and Barnabas when the going got rough and went back to mother (Acts 13:13). Now, twenty years later, the experience is woven into the fabric of the gospel and his understanding of it.

Alec McCowen took his solo presentation of Mark's gospel very seriously and dug deep in pursuit of its meaning. The message of this chapter could hardly be better summarised than in his words:

He has just told us.
'Only believe.'
This challenge has nagged for two thousand years.
We would prefer to build cathedrals, compose sacred masses, paint the Sistine Chapel. We would prefer to fast or fight crusades. We try to evade the ordinary words.
'Only believe.'
Stand up! Sit down! Wake up! Only believe!
ONLY?
Easier to fly to the moon.
(Alec McCowen, *Personal Mark*, Collins, 1984).

7

THE SYRO-PHOENICIAN WOMAN

[Mark 7:24–30]

[24]Jesus left that place and went to the vicinity of Tyre. He entered a house and did not want anyone to know it; yet he could not keep his presence secret. [25]In fact, as soon as she heard about him, a woman whose little daughter was possessed by an evil spirit came and fell at his feet. [26]The woman was a Greek, born in Syrian Phoenicia. She begged Jesus to drive the demon out of her daughter.

[27]"First let the children eat all they want," he told her, "for it is not right to take the children's bread and toss it to their dogs."

[28]"Yes, Lord," she replied, "but even the dogs under the table eat the children's crumbs."

[29]Then he told her, "For such a reply, you may go; the demon has left your daughter."

[30]She went home and found her child lying on the bed, and the demon gone.

The period between the raising of Jairus's daughter and this encounter with the Syro-Phoenician woman is dominated by travel and crowds. It includes a visit to Nazareth where he receives a lukewarm welcome, an extended teaching tour of the villages near by, a retrospective account of the arrest and execution of John the Baptist, the feeding of the five thousand, the walking on the water and an encounter with some Pharisees and teachers of the Law, who it seems had come down specially to assess the orthodoxy of this young rabbi.

The geography is, as usual in Mark's gospel, vague and obviously of little importance to him. Jesus goes 'from village

to village' (Mark 6:6), but Mark does not say to which villages
he went. The disciples are sent out on a missionary journey
without saying where they were sent. When they return, Jesus
takes them to an unidentified 'solitary place' where large
crowds of people, having heard of his presence there, gather
round him. When he has dismissed the crowds he goes into
the hills to pray, leaving the disciples to set off by boat to
Bethsaida. He joins the boat in mid-journey and they land at
Gennesaret, which is a fertile region on the western side of the
lake. There he is challenged by the Pharisees and some
teachers of the Law to account for his supposedly easy-going
practices. After the debate with them, he 'enters the house'
and then (7:24) Jesus left that place and went to the vicinity of
Tyre.

We are in no position to reconstruct these journeys accurately, and Mark certainly does not attempt to do so. He is
relying upon memories and reminiscences which, though no
doubt accurate in detail, are difficult to arrange in any
meaningful order. But there is a prevailing historical-
theological theme which it is important to understand ahead
of any study of the passage now in hand. The theme is one of
rejection and danger. He goes to his own home-town, which
Mark does not bother to name, and preaches in the synagogue. Conscious of his humble origin and the fact that his
relatives were still living in Nazareth, the people turn against
him, and all that he can do there is lay his hands on a few sick
people (6:5). It was this episode which provoked the saying –
'Only in his home town, among his relatives and in his own
house is a prophet without honour' (6:4). With this experience in mind he warns the disciples when he sends them out
on mission that 'if any place will not welcome you or listen to
you, shake the dust off your feet when you leave, as a
testimony against them' (6:11). He himself was in the process
of shaking the dust of Nazareth off his feet.

After the feeding of the five thousand, when Jesus joined
the disciples walking on the water, Mark records of the
disciples 'they were completely amazed, for they had not
understood about the loaves; their hearts were hardened'
(6:51–2). Thus even the disciples are exhibited in an adverse

light, being men of good will but conventional and obtuse. The subsequent encounter with the Pharisees and the teachers of the Law heightens the impression of growing opposition to everything that Jesus seemed to stand for.

By a literary convention, familiar in the ancient world, Mark interpolates into these intervening chapters the story of how John the Baptist had been arrested and beheaded by King Herod. He records that 'John's disciples came and took his body and laid it in a tomb' (6:29). There is something desperately and deliberately final about those words; they represented in Mark's mind the utter quenching of the hope of Israel. The last and greatest of the prophets is dead and buried, executed by the hand of a son of Herod the Great.

But the passage begins with an ominous note – 'King Herod heard about this, for Jesus' name had become well known' (6:14). It is evident that Jesus's fame had reached even into Herod's court and that he was a subject of conversation there. To be a subject of conversation in Herod's court was to be in danger of arrest and execution by this quixotic princeling. So it was becoming increasingly true that the Son of Man had nowhere safely to lay his head – criticised by his own family, rejected in his own town, criticised by the official leaders of Judaism, and now under threat from the political authorities. It is in this context that Mark records, without explanation or comment, that 'Jesus left that place and went to the vicinity of Tyre' (7:24). The significance of this journey is lost on us unless we appreciate the reputation of Tyre, and its surroundings both in the world and in the life of Israel.

Tyre

To the Hebrews, Tyre and its associated city of Sidon were locations on the other side of their northern boundary – just as Englishmen used to think of Europe as the other side of the English Channel. But Tyre was by any standards an infinitely more important place than anything within the boundaries of Israel. It was built on an island just off the coast with a deep-water harbour capable of handling the largest ships of the ancient world, and with what we could call today an impressive infrastructure of docks and warehouses, stimulated by the rich flow of exports from the hinterland of Syria to the whole of the Mediterranean world.

It was like nineteenth-century Liverpool, which attracted and produced great wealth and played an important part in international history. The Phoenicians were colonisers in much the same sense as the British were later to be. They had learnt the art of what we now call astro-navigation and they thus enjoyed a huge advantage over their commercial rivals by being able to sail continuously while other fleets could only proceed by hugging the land and anchoring at night. On the strength of this superiority they founded trading colonies all round the Mediterranean, the most famous of which was to be Carthage, just west of Tunis in what we now call Libya.

It was founded from Tyre in 814 BC and became strong enough in the course of the centuries to challenge even the power of Rome. The great Carthaginian general, Hannibal (247–183 BC) came near to a total victory over Rome. So Tyre was not just another coastal town on the other side of Israel's northern boundary: it was the birthplace and heart of an extensive imperial system, and was viewed by the earlier Hebrews with a mixture of awe and contempt – awe, because of its size and importance, contempt, because of the corruption which resulted from its trading eminence. Ezekiel particularly among the prophets was eloquent in his condemnations. Of many passages this one is typical:

> The word of the Lord came to me: "Son of man, say to the ruler of Tyre, 'This is what the Sovereign Lord says:
> "'In the pride of your heart you say, "I am a god; I sit on the throne of a god in the heart of the seas." But you are a man and not a god, though you think you are as wise as a god.
> Are you wiser than Daniel? Is no secret hidden from you? By your wisdom and understanding you have gained wealth for yourself and amassed gold and silver in your treasuries. By your great skill in trading you have increased your wealth, and because of your wealth your heart has grown proud.
> "'Therefore this is what the Sovereign Lord says:
> "'Because you think you are wise, as wise as a god, I am going to

bring foreigners against you, the most ruthless of nations; they will draw their swords against your beauty and wisdom and pierce your shining splendour.

They will bring you down to the pit, and you will die a violent death in the heart of the seas.

Will you then say, "I am a god," in the presence of those who kill you?

You will be but a man, not a god, in the hands of those who slay you.

You will die the death of the uncircumcised at the hands of foreigners.

I have spoken, declares the Sovereign Lord."
(Ezek. 28:1–10)

To have to record, therefore, that the long-awaited Messiah of Israel could leave the Holy Land and stay in Tyre must have caused Mark to think furiously. So astonishing was it to Luke, if he was aware of the incident, that he did not record it at all. It is one of the curiosities of the New Testament that Luke omits the whole of what we have come to call the Gentile section of Mark, viz. 6:45–8:26, either because he did not have access to this particular section of Mark, or because there were elements in this section which he perceived would be grossly offensive to other Gentiles like himself. Perhaps he did not care for the remark about Gentile dogs.

But even Matthew, who does follow Mark here, qualifies the story in certain important details. For example, he suggests that the woman came from the vicinity of Tyre and Sidon, which leaves open the option that Jesus did not actually go into the city himself (Matt. 15:22). Moreover, in Matthew's account, Jesus seems to enunciate a general principle when he says, in response to the woman's request, 'I was sent only to the lost sheep of Israel' (v. 24). This is another instance of how important it is to isolate Mark from the other evangelists when we are trying to establish what Mark himself had in mind and what he meant.

Read without the advantage of our knowledge of Matthew, the narrative is striking. Jesus went to Tyre, leaving, so it seems, his disciples behind him in Galilee, and even entered a house there. This would be no great problem to the reader because there were Jews living in Tyre as there were in every other major city in the ancient world. It has to be supposed that Jesus found lodging in a Jewish home. There is no indication of how long he stayed there or what else he did in the city.

If the Johannine chronology of a ministry of three years is the correct one then there is room in the chronology for a stay of several months – over which there is a veil of silence. The woman, so Mark says, was a Greek, which could mean that she spoke Greek or that she was just a Gentile, but she is more closely identified by being called a Syro-Phoenician to distinguish her from a Libya-Phoenician, who were of the same race but dwelt on the African seaboard. So she was far from being 'one of the lost sheep of the house of Israel'. She was as far removed from the covenant of grace as any person could be, and in speaking to her Jesus was breaking every rule in the book – speaking to a woman while on his own, and consorting with the representative of a religion which Israel abhorred for its idolatry, corruption and its practice of human sacrifice. The only aspect of the conversation of which a loyal Jew would have approved would have been the proverb which Jesus quoted – 'It is not right to take the children's bread and toss it to the dogs.'

It was this attitude which is reflected by St Paul when he reverses the traditional roles of Hebrews and pagans in the ancient world when he says 'watch out for those dogs', referring to the Jewish adversaries of his mission (Phil. 3:2). The dénouement is extraordinary. It would have seemed extraordinary not only to Jesus but to his disciples if they had been there. The woman persists, makes a witty response acknowledging her racial inferiority, but pressing her case just the same, and is rewarded with the announcement that she can go home because her daughter is better.

What did it mean to Mark?

It is a good principle of biblical study always to ask three questions about any book or any particular passage, viz.: What did it mean to the author as he recorded it? What did it mean to those who read it or heard it? What did it mean to the participants? There is no way of achieving a balanced view of any incident except on these terms. We have to ask this question, therefore: What did this passage mean to Mark, assuming that he had no one looking over his shoulder to tell him what it meant?

Mark had been a companion of St Paul, and had been involved in the bitter controversies between Jew and Gentile which in Paul's view severely hampered the mission he had been given. As we have seen, so exasperated did he occasionally become that he uses distinctly undiplomatic words of his countrymen – those 'dogs' who were undermining his work, seeking to impose the Law of Moses in all its rigor on the new converts in Philippi. This was an oft-repeated pattern: reverberations of the dispute can be heard throughout the Acts of the Apostles. Mark could hardly have been unaware of that controversy when he recorded this incident in Tyre.

Here was Jesus himself staying in heathen territory, speaking to a woman, bringing the grace of God to someone who had no claim on him by virtue of birth or religion. There could hardly have been a clearer endorsement of that mission to which Paul had been called and on which he had been so energetically engaged. Paul had been sent 'far away to the Gentiles' in Greece and Rome (Acts 22:21); Jesus had been sent by the same God far away among the Gentiles in Tyre and Sidon. In Mark's view Jesus's journey to Tyre and Sidon was no impulse, engendered only by the opposition of the Jews or by Herod's antipathy, but an act of obedience to the call of God himself. For Mark, what he was recording in his own matter-of-fact way was the beginning of the mission to the Gentiles.

What did it mean to the early Church?

And so it would have seemed to those who heard the gospel read, the little Christian assemblies of the early Church where

Jewish and Gentile Christians met together for worship. Mark was writing, and the people would have been listening, at a time of acute unrest in the ancient world.

In AD 66 began the first Jewish revolt, and echoes of it would soon have reached Jews and Christians in the capital, Rome. They would have heard of towns being captured by Jews in Israel itself. They would have heard of Jews being massacred by Gentiles. They might even have shared the official view that it was a general, premeditated revolt by Jews all over the world, and not just in Palestine itself. Tension, therefore, between Jew and Gentile was at its height when Mark wrote and his hearers listened to the gospel in the second half of the sixties.

What was to be their attitude to each other, therefore, in these little mixed communities of Jews and Gentiles united by a common faith in Jesus of Nazareth? The answer was clear if, as so often in ecclesiastical matters, the implications were less than obvious. If this encounter between Jesus and the Syro-Phoenician woman really happened as Mark said it did, then their allegiance to Jesus must transcend any differences which arise out of differing religious or racial associations. The call of God to those little assemblies in Greece and Rome was clear, as it had been to Paul, and as it had been to Jesus himself. When Jesus left the boundaries of Israel and went to Tyre, he stepped on to the world stage. He could no longer be regarded just as the Jewish Messiah because he was to be, in John's words, the Saviour of the world.

What did it mean to Jesus?

We turn now to the third question: What did the incident mean to Jesus himself? This of course permits no easy answer, and we are on our own, just as Mark was on his own when he recorded it. But even if we cannot hope for an assured answer, just to ask the question is to permit the entrance of God's Word at the point where human thought and specu-lation necessarily falter. The claim to be able to trace the psychological history of Jesus has long been discredited. The

New Testament does not provide the data for doing so, and the evangelists were plainly not interested in uncovering the inner life of their subject. There are clues in John's gospel, but they remain only clues, isolated from each other without any systematic form.

But although the claim to provide an authoritative account of our Lord's inner life must be disowned, it is difficult for a twentieth-century man not to speculate on the inner process which went on behind the plain accounts which are provided by the evangelists. The fact that Jesus is now depicted in stained-glass windows, presented in painting and sculpture, honoured in a long tradition of music, the object of veneration and worship by a third of the human race, does not alter the fact that Jesus was a human being, whatever else he may have been. A human being without inner thoughts, questionings, without secret aspirations and hopes and fears, without a growing awareness born of circumstances, without an inner history, is scarcely a human being as we understand such.

The writer of the letter to the Hebrews says that Jesus learned obedience by the things he suffered (Heb. 5:8) – and that does not simply refer to the things he suffered in the Garden of Gethsemane, at Pilate's court-house, or on Calvary. His suffering was the inner unseen cost of seeking at every moment of every day to learn and to do the will of God regardless of his own feelings, his own opinion, his own temperament. And when that inner obedience is faced with the disbelief, the lukewarmness, sometimes the plain hostility of those around him, we begin to get a sense of what is meant by: 'He learned obedience by the things he suffered.' It was the total accommodation of his own will to the will of his Father in heaven which makes him, so we believe, unique in the history of the world.

If we ask the question, therefore, 'Why did he go to Tyre?' the answer must be that it was in accordance with the will of God that he should do so. No less than three times Paul recounted the story of the vision of God which sent him out far away among the Gentiles. With Jesus, on the other hand, we have no means of knowing how he became convinced that

he was to leave Galilee behind and go to Tyre; disappoint-
ment with the reaction of his own people or fear of Herod
would certainly not of themselves have provoked such an
action. He was being sent far away among the Gentiles by 'the
determinate counsel and foreknowledge of God', and he
bowed to God's decree.

But then what did the incident recorded here mean to him?
What did he learn from it? This is one of the few encounters in
the gospels in which the encounter probably meant more to
Jesus than it did even to the woman whose daughter was
healed. Jesus had not sought the encounter and was clearly
unprepared for it. He had gone there for some undisclosed
reason to be, for a time at least, on his own, away from the
pressures of public life. The meeting was in that sense
'accidental'; there was no briefing on his desk to prepare him
for the interview.

Jesus was a Jew and he would have shared the racial
prejudices of his people. It was no light thing to travel in the
region of Tyre and Sidon. The inhabitants of that land
enjoyed an evil reputation for cruelty and vice, and their
forefathers, the Canaanites, were among the earliest enemies
of Israel. There was no reason, humanly speaking, to suppose
that he was going to be accosted by a Syro-Phoenician woman
in search of healing for her daughter. But it happened, and a
decision was required of him. This is where we may legit-
imately call on the resources of the fourth gospel where a very
similar incident is recorded in chapter 4.

Pursuing the more direct route from Jerusalem to Galilee
through Samaria, Jesus stopped at Jacob's Well near Sychar
where a woman from the town came to draw water. This was
another unsought interview which exposed the inner needs
and aspirations of the woman herself and presented Jesus,
too, with a challenge. The Jews had no dealings with Samaritans (John 4:9). The woman was surprised that he was
prepared to talk with her. The outcome of the interview was
enthusiastic witness and faith on her part and the conversion
of many of the Samaritans in her town. The heart of the
interview is revealed in the following section:

Jesus declared, 'Believe me, woman, a time is coming when you will worship the Father neither on this mountain nor in Jerusalem. You Samaritans worship what you do not know; we worship what we do know, for salvation is from the Jews. Yet a time is coming and has now come when the true worshippers will worship the Father in spirit and in truth, for they are the kind of worshippers the Father seeks. God is spirit, and his worshippers must worship in spirit and in truth'. (John 4:21–4)

The encounter with the Samaritan woman caused Jesus to articulate for her sake what must have been a growing conviction in his own mind – the day was at hand when sectarian conflict and racial division would be transcended by the universal reign of God and the universal worship of him. If it was true that Jews had no dealings with Samaritans who were related to them, and who honoured the Pentateuch, it was certainly true that the Jews had no dealings with Syro-Phoenicians.

Thus the case is much more extreme in Mark than in St John, and the decision that much more critical. The Syro-Phoenician woman's response to Jesus left him no way out: he was called to be Lord of the Gentiles, or he was not. He was to be the Saviour of the world, not just of Israel. The future of the world depended on his reaction. Angels kept silence in heaven while the issue of the day was fought out on earth. The fate of mankind trembled in the balance. He had gone to Tyre for a holiday; he stayed to found a Kingdom. The young Jewish tradesman, alienated from his family, rejected by his own people, disowned by the religious authorities, at risk from the political ruler of the land, had discovered in Tyre the meaning of his mission and God's long-term objective for the whole world.

There is one pregnant phrase in Mark's account which means more to Mark than we might suppose: 'He entered a house and did not want anyone to know it yet he could not keep his presence secret' (7:24). In Jesus the Syro-Phoenician woman discerned the presence of God himself. He could not be hidden even in the teeming streets and amid the busy markets of one of the great cities of the Levant. It was a point well made by a Scottish divine of the earlier part of this century, G. H. Morrison, in his book, *The Return of the Angels*. He is commenting on this passage:

> Every letter you write you date from Jesus. Commerce is vast and intricate and keen, yet commerce ceases the day when Jesus rose. On every hospital Christ is written large. On every orphanage His name is graven. Through every provision for the friendless and the fallen, the pity of His heart is shining still. Think what you will of Christ, there is the fact, that history has been powerless to hide Him. You cannot avoid Him; He confronts you everywhere; He is magnificently and universally conspicuous. And yet this Christ was very meek and lowly, and shrunk from popularity and clamour. (Hodder & Stoughton, 1909).

Mark could not have said it so eloquently, but he would have said 'Amen' to it.

8

THE BLIND MAN AT BETHSAIDA

[Mark 8:22–6]

[22]They came to Bethsaida, and some people brought a blind man and begged Jesus to touch him. [23]He took the blind man by the hand and led him outside the village. When he had spat on the man's eyes and put his hands on him, Jesus asked, "Do you see anything?"

[24]He looked up and said, "I see people; they look like trees walking around."

[25]Once more Jesus put his hands on the man's eyes. Then his eyes were opened, his sight was restored, and he saw everything clearly. [26]Jesus sent him home, saying, "Don't go into the village."

If the geographical allusions of the previous section were vague, in this section they are almost impenetrable. After the encounter with the Syro-Phoenician woman Mark records that 'Jesus left the vicinity of Tyre and went through Sidon, down to the Sea of Galilee and into the region of the Decapolis' (Mark 7:31). Even a casual glance at a map will show you how remarkable that itinerary was. If Mark means what he says, it would have required Jesus to make a journey of some forty miles northwards to Sidon, then a route eastwards towards Damascus at the foot of Mount Lebanon, then a journey south along the eastern side of the Jordan to the eastern bank of the Sea of Galilee among the towns of the Decapolis. Some scholars have suggested that it is like going from Cornwall to London via Manchester. But it might be nearer to scale to say that it was like a journey from London to

Oxford and then to Banbury, and then back to London via Cambridge.

By whatever route, it was a longish journey of two hundred miles or more, and that – as we have constantly to remind ourselves – on foot, in inhospitable country, on roads only too commonly infested with robbers. The only thing that can be said with certainty about the route is that Jesus studiously avoided Galilee. Back in the Decapolis Jesus is once more confronted with the crowds, and a man is brought to him who was deaf and dumb. The healing is described, and the incident ends in the amazement of the people, who said 'He has done everything well . . . He even makes the deaf hear and the mute speak' (Mark 7:37).

This is followed by the feeding of the four thousand which is often regarded as a doublet of the previous feeding of the five thousand. But it is significantly different in form and location, and whereas the previous feeding was indubitably in Jewish territory, this one is in Gentile territory. This is followed by a journey across the lake by boat to the region of Dalmanutha.

The name Dalmanutha is unknown to us, and may well have been unknown to Matthew, who substitutes for it 'the vicinity of Magadan' (Matt. 15:39). The whereabouts of Magadan may have been known to Matthew, but unfortunately it is not known to us. Some texts of Matthew therefore read 'Magdala', birthplace of Mary Magdalene, which is on the west shore of the lake. Even if we cannot exactly locate the place, the inference is that Jesus went in the boat to the other side of the lake and once more (and for the last time) into Galilee.

When he landed there, almost as if his movements were known in advance, he was met by the Pharisees, asking him for a sign from heaven. There is a strong emotional tone to Jesus's reply: 'He sighed deeply, and said, "Why does this generation ask for a miraculous sign? I tell you the truth, no sign will be given to it"' (Mark 8:12). So his voyage is resumed and he sailed to Bethsaida, which is in the territory of Philip the tetrarch.

Opposition

These random journeys, which must indeed have seemed random even to Mark as he recorded them, call for some explanation. If we ignore the chapter divisions which are modern and bear little relationship to the structure of the gospel, we may observe that the whole 'Gentile section', so called, is framed by recurring disputes with the Pharisees. It was after a long argument with the Pharisees (Mark 7:1–14) that Jesus left Galilee and went to Tyre. And now, as a result of a sudden excursion to Galilee, he is confronted once more by the Pharisees seeking for a sign from heaven (Mark 8:11–13).

This framework may well be much more significant to our understanding of the gospel than a knowledge of the exact itinerary. Having originally left Galilee to avoid the attentions of his opponents, he now returns after several months and finds that the opposition is as vindictive and hostile as ever. The exact details of the itinerary may well be irrecoverable, but the whole section is dominated by the well-orchestrated opposition of the official leaders of Israel which made any further ministry in Herod's territory impossible. These random journeys look more like the journeys of a hunted man, aware of the risks that attended every public appearance. It was becoming increasingly true that he had nowhere to lay his head safely.

Tension with the Pharisees

This whole section is headed in the New English Bible 'growing tension', and that is an apt description. The signs of tension are there in his encounters with the Pharisees – those 'hypocrites' as he calls them (Mark 7:6). They are there in his encounter with the Syro-Phoenician woman as we have seen. They are there in his renewed dispute with the Pharisees after the feeding of the four thousand.

The word which is translated 'sighed deeply' is used only here in the New Testament, and it is a word intended to

suggest deep perturbation of spirit. Why, we may ask? The
Pharisees were demanding a sign from heaven to establish
Jesus's credentials. They were not satisfied with the casting
out of demons and the healing of the sick. These were mere
signs on earth, for there were many other exorcists and
healers abroad.

They wanted an unmistakable signal from heaven, a demonstration of divine power written across the sky. They
wanted to hear the voice of God himself authenticating his
ministry. It was not sufficient to know that the Kingdom of
Heaven was at hand, they wanted to see it and to be able to
report their observations at head office in Jerusalem. It was
this demand which created the emotional upheaval in Jesus's
mind. He was confident by now of his vocation from God; he
was reassured by the testimony of John the Baptist; he had
heard the voice of God himself by the River Jordan saying,
'You are my Son, whom I love; with you I am well pleased'
(Mark 1:11); he had proved the resources of almighty God in
his own prodigious acts of healing, not least in the raising of
the dead.

But here were the official leaders of his people disowning
him and eager to destroy him. No phenomenon in the sky
would prove anything to these hardened sceptics. It is in this
general context that we need to understand the so-called 'sin
against the Holy Spirit' which arose out of a previous dispute
with the teachers of the Law:

> So Jesus called them and spoke to them in parables: 'How can
> Satan drive out Satan? If a kingdom is divided against itself, that
> kingdom cannot stand. If a house is divided against itself, that
> house cannot stand. And if Satan opposes himself and is divided,
> he cannot stand; his end has come. In fact no-one can enter a
> strong man's house and carry off his possessions unless he first
> ties up the strong man. Then he can rob his house. I tell you the
> truth, all the sins and blasphemies of men will be forgiven them.
> But whoever blasphemes against the Holy Spirit will never be
> forgiven; he is guilty of eternal sin'. He said this because they
> were saying, 'He has an evil spirit'. (Mark 3:23–30)

There was no more Jesus could do. He re-embarked and returned to the other side of the lake. The die was cast; he would never return to Galilee again until he came in triumph after his resurrection.

Tensions with Jesus's disciples

But there are signs of tension elsewhere than in his relationship with the leaders of Israel. The section is marked not only by disputes with them, but with misunderstandings between Jesus and his disciples.

After the feeding of the five thousand when Jesus joined them in the boat and the wind died down (Mark 6:51), they were, Mark says, 'completely amazed, for they had not understood about the loaves; their hearts were hardened.' After the dispute with the Pharisees, on their journey back to Bethsaida, Mark records that the disciples had forgotten to bring bread and when they heard our Lord saying, 'Watch out for the yeast of the Pharisees and that of Herod' (Mark 8:15), they assumed that they were being rebuked for their oversight in not bringing bread.

It provoked the sharpest response recorded so far in Jesus's attitude to the disciples: 'Do you still not see or understand? Are your hearts hardened? Do you have eyes but fail to see, and ears but fail to hear?' (Mark 8:17–18). It was bad enough to be threatened by his enemies; it was even worse to be misunderstood by his friends.

They had been with him now for many months. They had shared in his daily life and had been witnesses of some of the most amazing events. They had seen the sick healed and the dead raised, the devils cast out. They had, with their own hands, distributed an abundance of bread to the crowds from their own tiny resources of bread and fish – but in their heavy, pedestrian way they had quite failed to see the significance of these events. For them the whole thing was a highly gratifying exercise in public relations; they had left their fishing-nets and their customs office and were now in the public eye. They were thrilled with the success of their Master; they were waiting for something really big to happen. The Kingdom was at hand, and would break in upon a startled world at any moment – and they would be on twelve thrones judging the twelve tribes of Israel. It was a strange amalgam of superstition, excitement, and a genuine devotion to Jesus which as yet had yielded no conception of who he was or why he was here.

Tension in Jesus's mind

No doubt both these factors – the opposition of the Pharisees and the slowness of his disciples – were a cause of growing tension in Jesus's own mind. He at that moment did not see the distant future. He did not look down the long vistas of time to the majestic churches to be raised in his name, the ravishing music to be sung in his honour, the books that would be written about him, the conquests his Church would make. At that moment he was just a lonely man from a lowly background, with no access to the corridors of power, no protection from the mighty, with no home of his own and no settled programme for the future. Everything depended as far as he could see, on the willingness of his few followers to believe the unbelievable and to think the unthinkable.

He had lived with his divine vocation now for several years. There was no doubt in his own mind about the importance of that to which he had been called. He had received ample evidence of the mighty power of God working in him. But now he was little more than a fugitive, likely to share the fate of his kinsman, John the Baptist, with all the forces of the world arrayed against him.

Perhaps already images of the suffering servant described in Isaiah 53 were rising before his eyes. With all the horrific possibilities for himself – wounded, bruised, chastised, executed (Isa. 53:4–9). That had been the fate of the true prophets of Israel often enough: perhaps it was to be his fate. Yet there could be hope the other side of dread, or perhaps, like the suffering servant, he would see the fruit of the travail of his soul and be satisfied (Isa. 53:11). The reader of the gospel needs to become aware of the sheer isolation and the

inner turmoil which are so characteristic of Mark's portrait of
Jesus. The gospel is almost inexplicable without that awareness.

An unusual miracle of healing

It is in this setting of 'growing tension' that the healing of the
blind man at Bethsaida needs to be understood. Mark refers
to Bethsaida as a village. Scholars will tell you that Bethsaida
was a large and flourishing town built by Philip the tetrarch in
honour of Julia, the daughter of Augustus. However, the
scholars will also say that the city was built at some little
distance from the shore, and that the original fishing village
remained. We must presume that it was here that the healing
of the blind man took place.

There are one or two remarkable features of this healing.
The first is that it is not recorded by the other evangelists at
all. That is not surprising in St Luke's case because the whole
'Gentile section' is omitted from his narrative, but it is
surprising in the case of Matthew because, on the whole, he
follows the Marcan outline faithfully. There is no reason to
suppose that he did not have this episode in the copy of the
gospel in front of him. Perhaps he omitted it, either because
he did not understand it himself, or because he thought it
could be misunderstood by his readers in the latter half of the
first century.

He may not have understood, for example, why the blind
man was so categorically sent home, but told not to go into the
village. He may not have liked the therapeutic method involved (spitting on the man's eyes) which smacked more of
the magician than of the divine son of God on earth. Or it
could have been because he did not see the point of this
gradual healing, which makes the miracle distinct from all the
others.

And yet, perhaps, this was just the point. Perhaps this
stood in Jesus's mind not just for the gradual healing of a blind
man who crossed his path in Bethsaida, but for the gradual
opening of the eyes of his disciples. For all their slowness of

mind and hardness of heart perhaps the light was dawning. Could it be that they were beginning to see things like 'trees walking around', and might soon see him as he really was?

It is no accident that the healing of the blind man at Bethsaida immediately precedes Peter's confession of Christ recorded in the next section. The two events are closely related in Mark's mind, and they interpret each other. Perhaps this was just the message Jesus himself needed in his own anxieties and confusions. Perhaps the healing of the blind man was an acted parable given by God's grace, a sign of the coming illumination of the disciples and the consummation of Jesus's ministry amongst them.

The word 'perhaps' occurs all too often in this paragraph. But uncertainty in matters of detail is one of the facts of life which the reader has to accept. It is probable that Mark knew more than he recorded. It is possible that he did not always understand the significance of what he recorded. He had not been there at the time, and was wholly dependent on the scattered reminiscences of Peter and the other apostles. The apostles may not have seen the significance of the events in which they were involved until much later.

Suffering servants of God

Opposition and misunderstanding had been the fate of the prophets from Moses onwards. The wilderness wanderings of Israel are punctuated by the people's reluctance to accept Moses' authority and sometimes by downright rebellion. When he goes into the mountain to receive the Law of God the people break loose and, with Aaron's connivance, make a golden calf. They grumbled at the hardships of the desert and were only too ready to turn back to the fleshpots of Egypt. They were intimidated by the thought of the dangers that awaited them in the Promised Land and spurned the heritage which God had provided for them.

Moses was a 'suffering servant', suffering the opposition, the ingratitude and the blind stupidity of the people of whom God had given him charge. The pattern is repeated almost

without exception in the lives of all the great prophets. The
following words are attached in the text to the story of Isaiah's
vision of God in the Temple:

> He said, 'Go and tell this people: "Be ever hearing, but never
> understanding; be ever seeing, but never perceiving." Make the
> heart of this people calloused; make their ears dull and close their
> eyes. Otherwise they might see with their eyes, hear with their
> ears, understand with their hearts, and turn and be healed.'
> (Isaiah 6:9–10)

These words, although actually recorded at the beginning of
his ministry, may reflect the fruits of Isaiah's later experience.
He had found the people 'hard of heart, with their ears dull
and their eyes closed'. The author of the Wisdom of Solomon,
much nearer the time of Christ, observed the same tendency
in his people:

> Let us lay a trap for the just man; he stands in our way, a check to
> us at every turn; he girds at us as law-breakers, and calls us
> traitors to our upbringing. He knows God, so he says; he styles
> himself 'the servant of the Lord'. He is a living condemnation of
> all our ideas. The very sight of him is an affliction to us, because
> his life is not like other people's, and his ways are different. He
> rejects us like base coin, and avoids us and our ways as if we were
> filth; he says that the just die happy, and boasts that God is his
> father. Let us test the truth of his words, let us see what will
> happen to him in the end; for if the just man is God's son, God
> will stretch out a hand to him and save him from the clutches of
> his enemies. Outrage and torment are the means to try him with,
> to measure his forbearance and learn how long his patience
> lasts. Let us condemn him to a shameful death, for on his own
> showing he will have a protector.
> So they argued, and very wrong they were; blinded by their
> own malevolence, they did not understand God's hidden plan.
> They never expected that holiness of life would have its re-
> compense; they thought that innocence had no reward. (Wisd. of
> Sol. 2:12–22 NEB)

So Jesus in his conflict with the religious leaders of his day and
in the misunderstandings of his followers stood in a familiar

prophetic tradition. Incomprehension, not just downright
wickedness, is the heaviest burden that the man of God has to
bear.

The Mystery

The reader of the gospel cannot afford to be too con-
temptuous of the Pharisees or too critical of the disciples.
Both groups were reacting to an unprecedented event; the
Pharisees were no doubt genuinely concerned for the survival
and integrity of Israel; the disciples were just out of their
depth. Even the wise and the learned ever since have been out
of their depth. There is a mystery at the heart of Jesus which
the mind of man has never plumbed. The mystics and the
saints have occasionally drawn near to that mystery and have
fallen back baffled before it. Even the greatest of the sons of
men, like the blind man of Bethsaida, have – at least in this life
– to be content with seeing trees walking. But that gradual
recovery of sight in Bethsaida is luminous with promise for
the future. The word translated 'clearly' is found only here in
the New Testament, and it is a dramatic word meaning
dazzling brilliance – the rapturous experience of the man who
sees for the first time in his life. Now we see through a glass,
darkly, then face to face.

9

SIMON PETER

[Mark 8:27–9:1]

[27]Jesus and his disciples went on to the villages around Caesarea Philippi. On the way he asked them, "Who do people say I am?"

[28]They replied, "Some say John the Baptist; others say Elijah; and still others, one of the prophets."

[29]"But what about you?" he asked. "Who do you say I am?"

Peter answered, "You are the Christ."

[30]Jesus warned them not to tell anyone about him.

[31]He then began to teach them that the Son of Man must suffer many things and be rejected by the elders, chief priests and teachers of the law, and that he must be killed and after three days rise again. [32]He spoke plainly about this, and Peter took him aside and began to rebuke him.

[33]But when Jesus turned and looked at his disciples, he rebuked Peter. "Get behind me, Satan!" he said. "You do not have in mind the things of God, but the things of men."

[34]Then he called the crowd to him along with his disciples and said: "If anyone would come after me, he must deny himself and take up his cross and follow me. [35]For whoever wants to save his life will lose it, but whoever loses his life for me and for the gospel will save it. [36]What good is it for a man to gain the whole world, yet forfeit his soul? [37]Or what can a man give in exchange for his soul? [38]If anyone is ashamed of me and my words in this adulterous and sinful generation, the Son of Man will be ashamed of him when he comes in his Father's glory with the holy angels."

9 And he said to them, "I tell you the truth, some who are standing here will not taste death before they see the kingdom of God come with power."

The gradual healing of the blind man of Bethsaida may be taken as a sign to Jesus himself of the gradual opening of the disciples' eyes to the nature and role of the person with whom they had companied for the previous three years. But the dénouement is not yet. For the moment Jesus remains a refugee, rejected by his own kinsfolk and by the people of Galilee, and subject to the implacable hostility of the religious leaders of Judah. So he remains outside the territory of Herod and keeps his distance from the religious authorities in Jerusalem. From Bethsaida, therefore, he travelled between twenty and thirty miles to 'the villages around Caesarea Philippi'.

Caesarea Philippi

It must have seemed to his followers a puzzling decision by their Master. The town and the territory around it had been given to Herod the Great by Caesar Augustus, and Herod, in gratitude for the gift, built a temple there in honour of Augustus. Philip the tetrarch, who inherited it, enlarged the town and richly embellished it, giving it his own name to distinguish it from the other Caesarea, the centre of Roman administration, on the coast of Palestine.

The town was at the source of the River Jordan at the foot of the slopes of Mount Hermon, and it had long been re-garded as a sacred site. The original deities of Canaan had been worshipped there, and subsequently it was dedicated to Pan, the great god of flocks and shepherds among the Greeks. We derive our word 'panic' from him because of the awe and terror he was supposed to induce among travellers. Great Pan was by no means dead at the time of Jesus and worship was offered to him in what was originally known as Paneas, later corrupted to Banias. Those who are familiar with the site will find it easy to understand why it had achieved such an aura of sanctity, and it is easy to see why Herod the Great should have found it politic to build a temple to Augustus there.

So the place had what we might call a certain 'ecumenical' dimension honoured by a variety of people for a variety of reasons – none of which would have appealed to the Jews in general or to the disciples in particular. It all smacked of the most arrant heathenism. Their only previous connection with it would have been the encounter between Jesus and the woman with the issue of blood, who, it is said, came from this area. The journey therefore must have seemed to them singularly purposeless, and yet it proved to be the scene in which an encounter took place which was to become the bedrock of the Church. A place which was sacred to the memory of Pan and a symbol of the divine honours which the Caesar received there is now a tourist attraction which countless people visit every year as one of the places in Israel sanctified in their minds by a visit of a little group of men from Galilee. Many of the people who visit it now have scarcely heard of Pan or of Augustus. It is the name of Christ which draws them there.

The Encounter

The encounter itself, so influential in its consequences for the world, is recorded with the utmost economy. Nothing is said of what Jesus did in the villages around Caesarea Philippi, or why he went there; no mighty works are recorded, no crowds gather at his door. Nature does not intervene with a sign from heaven or a sign on earth – no earthquake, no rushing mighty wind, no fire. The birth of a new age is described in seven sentences. Compare the amount of space in the average newspaper devoted to a trifling political decision or an unimportant domestic event, or even the result of a boxing match.

It is essential in reading the gospels to put 'space' round the words that are said or the events that are described. If Mark is taken literally none of Jesus's conversations ever lasted more than a couple of minutes. We have to imagine, therefore, in this instance, a conversation which may have lasted intermittently over several days, in which Jesus sought to probe and prompt the minds of his disciples. Perhaps they had talked together about some of the great prophets of old, what they did, and what they stood for; perhaps they discussed certain aspects of Israel's history; they could hardly have come to Banias without noticing the scenery at the foot of Mount Hermon and reflecting on the temple built to Augustus, and the sacred grotto in which Pan was worshipped.

Writing in the ancient world was a laborious process and writing material was costly. Mark had no time for such interesting digressions; he was writing a gospel, offering a view of Jesus for those who worshipped him in the early Church, providing brief cameos on which a view of Jesus and his disciples could be constructed. We need repeatedly to take note of the aphorism that Mark knew much more than he actually recorded.

As twentieth-century people, interested in personalities and characters and psychological growth, we may regret his omissions, but we must honour him for the precision of his writing and for the steadiness of his purpose. The whole meaning of the passage hinges on two expressions in the narrative, and it is to these that we now turn because of their importance in the vocabulary of the Jewish people and subsequently in the vocabulary of the Christian Church.

The Christ

The word 'Christ' has almost become a proper name in modern usage, as if to distinguish Jesus of the gospels from many others in his time who bore that familiar name (a Graecised version of 'Joshua'). But the word has a distinct meaning which is alternatively rendered in the NIV 'the Messiah' and 'the anointed one'. It derives from a word which means 'anoint' and it appears many times in its Hebrew form, especially in the books of Samuel, Kings and the Psalter. Most of the occurrences of the word are connected with the anointing of the king of Israel, which was part of standard coronation ceremonial.

Prior to the foundation of the monarchy it was used for the anointing of priests, but it becomes more and more exclusively associated with the monarchy after the occupation of

Palestine. So the prophet Samuel anointed Saul as king, and subsequently David; and the alternative name of the king of Israel was 'the Lord's anointed'. It signified the accreditation by God of the man whom he had called to be king, and it implied an absolute obligation to observe the Law of God in his own person and to apply the Word of God in justice and mercy to the people for whom he was responsible. There was no electoral process for the appointment of Saul or of David; they were chosen of God, and kings subsequent to them incurred the same obligations to God himself.

It would be obvious to any reader of the Old Testament that few of the kings of Israel lived up to their obligations, despite the exhortations of the prophets. Too often they proved to be cruel or weak or both, self-seeking, greedy for power and property, indifferent to the needs of their subjects and strikingly incompetent in their conduct of political and international affairs. The books of Samuel and Kings reach their final form after the collapse of the monarchy and the deportation of the people, and the authors attributed both these disasters to the manifest failure of the kings to live up to their obligations as 'the Lord's anointed'.

After the return from exile, the role of government devolved upon a succession of Scribes and High Priests, often enough at odds with each other. This remained the situation in Jesus's own time, as is evident from the gospels. But the aspiration for the ideal king, sometimes prefigured in the Psalter, never died, and it is nowhere expressed more potently than in this passage from Isaiah 9:2, 6–7 familiar to many in the soaring music of Handel's *Messiah*.

The people walking in darkness have seen a great
light; on those living in the land of the shadow
of death a light has dawned.
For unto us a child is born, to us a son is given,
and the government will be on his shoulders.
And he will be called Wonderful Counsellor,
Mighty God, Everlasting Father, Prince of Peace.
Of the increase of his government and peace
there will be no end. He will reign on David's
throne and over his kingdom, establishing and

upholding it with justice and righteousness
from that time on and for ever. The zeal
of the Lord Almighty will accomplish this.

It is beside the point whether or not this is one of the original
oracles of Isaiah the prophet. What is certain is that it became
part of the prophetic literature and kept alive through the
centuries the hope of such a king. But observe that the
language of the oracle almost excludes the possibility of
fulfilment in terms of an actual, historical king. Thus the idea
is beginning to acquire a new dimension which transcends the
personal and political role of an actual monarch. Peter could
scarcely be expected to have in his mind such a concept as I
have described, but he is, even if inadvertently, seeing the
fulfilment of a long-standing and precious hope in the minds
of the race to which he belongs when he says – 'you are the
Lord's anointed'. When Handel named his oratorio 'The
Messiah' he was honouring the same hope of a glorious future
under 'the Wonderful Counsellor, Mighty God, Everlasting
Father, the Prince of Peace'.

The Messianic image projected by the oracle from Isaiah 9
had, however, long since given place in most Jewish minds to
a far less exalted view of the future. The Messianic era
became the objective of political groups in Israel who thought
of it in terms of political activism, revolution and military
conquest, by which the Christ would cast off the yoke of
Rome and create a new political and social entity within the
boundaries of ancient Israel.

There were many such Christs eager to perform that role,
as Jesus himself knew (Mark 13:22). Some were genuine
patriots, some were just desperadoes, but all of them went the
same way in the end – defeat, disillusionment and death.
Rome did not welcome 'Christs' any more than Herod the
Great did, or for that matter Herod Antipas, or the high
priests. 'Christs' were disturbers of the peace, enemies of
good order and government, dangerous hotheads who
threatened the sometimes fragile boundaries of the Roman
empire. Peter himself, a man of his time, a Galilean and a
patriot, would not have been immune to such ideas, and,

indeed, the disciples later in the gospel are shown to be harbouring similar ideas when they asked whether they could sit on his right hand and his left in glory (Mark 10:37).

Son of Man

Peter's avowal, welcome though it was to Jesus, had in it the seeds of a gross misunderstanding which would somehow need to be corrected. That is why Jesus immediately 'began to teach them that the Son of Man must suffer many things and be rejected by the elders, chief priests and teachers of the Law, and that he must be killed and after three days rise again' (Mark 8:31). This was not the kind of Messiah the people of Israel generally, or even the disciples, were looking for, and it is understandable that Peter should express revulsion at the idea, and seek to deflect his Master from it.

But in insisting on this view of his role, as he does on several occasions before they reach Jerusalem, Jesus was tapping another source of understanding, long buried beneath the frivolities of political power and revolutionary action. And that source is represented by the term 'the Son of Man', which calls for some explanation.

The term has given birth to many theories and many books – and heated arguments in academic circles. There is no way I can cover that ground in a book of this size, so I can do no more than offer an opinion, shared by many others, but certainly not conclusive or complete. The term 'Son of Man' in itself is almost meaningless. In the Aramaic language it was little more than a circumlocution for a man, a human being. It surfaces most prominently in the writings of Ezekiel where it occurs frequently in God's conversations with the prophet, who is called 'Son of Man' – no more than a way of saying 'you' or 'Ezekiel'.

But in the later literature of Israel, both within and outside the pages of the Bible, the term acquires a certain mysterious significance. The classic instance is to be found in the book Daniel in the account of a vision which the author saw 'in the first year of Belshazzar, king of Babylon'. It is as follows:

In my vision at night I looked, and there before me was one like a
son of man, coming with the clouds of heaven. He approached
the Ancient of Days and was led into his presence. He was given
authority, glory and sovereign power; all peoples, nations and
men of every language worshipped him. His dominion is an
everlasting dominion that will not pass away, and his kingdom is
one that will never be destroyed. (Dan. 7:13–14)

The passage needs to be read carefully. The vision is of one
who was 'like a son of man', and the suggestion is that this
figure like a son of man was brought before the God of heaven
and given in his own person, authority, glory and sovereign
power and an everlasting dominion that would not pass away.
Such a vision far transcended anything that would normally
have been associated with the old Messianic ideal. What is
envisaged here is no earthly monarch anointed by God to rule
over his people, Israel, but a figure like a son of man who is to
have universal dominion over all the world, and was to rule by
the appointment of God himself in heaven.

So when Jesus used the term 'Son of Man' in this conversation he was conjuring up an image of the future with which
perhaps the disciples would have been slightly familiar. But in
doing so he was associating the figure of Daniel's vision with
himself, a human being standing in front of them talking to
them, walking with them; the man they had known intimately
for nearly three years, whose family background they were
aware of, whose brothers and sisters they had met, who had
been a humble artisan in an undistinguished little town in
Galilee.

But then they had to be prepared for another somersault of
the mind, because this same figure, appointed by God as the
ruler of the world, was to endure torture, shame and death.
This would have been altogether too much for Peter, but in
his attempt to disown such a view of the Messiah, he incurs
one of the most savage rebukes ever received by anyone in the
gospels. Peter was making a satanic suggestion and is dismissed in the same words that Matthew uses in Jesus's
dismissal of Satan in the wilderness temptations (Matt. 4:10).

Mark's 'Gospel'

Mark is not just telling a story. He is proclaiming a gospel.
This particular encounter is a vivid illustration of that obvious
truth; it is, generally, devoid of the details of time and scene
which any historian or biographer would include as a matter
of course. Now is the time to ask what Mark's gospel is, and
why he is proclaiming it in the way that he does.

The gospel as it emerges from this incident at Caesarea
Philippi is that Jesus was the Messiah for whom the Jewish
people had been waiting, that he was opposed by his own
people, largely misunderstood by his own disciples, and was
ultimately crucified. But he was the Messiah, and his status in
God's plan for the world is vindicated by his resurrection from
the dead. This is what Mark says in his own unblinking way to
the Church to which he belonged.

But the story of the crucified Messiah has implications for
those who profess his name and belong to his Church. The
disciple is not above his master, and has to learn, like Peter,
the hard way that to follow such a Messiah is to incur the risk
of unpopularity, persecution and even martyrdom. The
account of Peter's reaction to Jesus's prophecy of arrest and
death is not just an item of history; it is a warning to would-be
disciples of Mark's own day that they cannot expect an easy
ride. Peter would like to have been a follower of a Messiah
who triumphed over his enemies and established a kingdom in
which he himself would have had pride of place. It was not to
be, and never would be.

Jesus's enemies triumphed over him and victory lay the
other side of unthinkable pain and dereliction. Mark had
learned this lesson well from his mentor, St Paul, that: 'We
must go through many hardships to enter the kingdom of
God' (Acts 14:22). Mark's gospel is good news for the weak
who know that they are weak. It is bad news for the weak who
think that they are strong. 'Who then can be saved?' the
disciples asked. Jesus replied, 'With man this is impossible,
but not with God; all things are possible with God' (Mark
10:26-7).

The Suffering Messiah

The incident at Caesarea Philippi brings to an end the erratic journeys and seeming confusions which had dominated the previous few months of Jesus's life. Even within the narrative it is possible to discern a certain sense of relief – relief that the disciples had avowed, however inadequately, their faith in him as Messiah, and relief that the die was now cast. Jesus had crossed the Rubicon and had set his feet on the path that was to lead to Jerusalem and to the climax of his life's work.

Of course, that climax as he began to see it was horrific, and Jesus would have been less than human (not more) if he had not shuddered at the prospect which lay ahead of him. But perhaps we could dare to say that he was now clear in his mind about the object of his calling and about the meaning of his life on earth. He was not another Elijah, or another Jeremiah, he was not John the Baptist returned from the dead, he was the Messiah, the long-awaited Saviour of Israel. But more than that, he was not just a son of Abraham, or a son of David, he was 'the Son of Man', to whom was to be given 'dominion and glory and a kingdom that all peoples, nations and languages should serve him (Dan. 7:14).

But this kingdom was not to be the consequence of successful political action or of a sudden change of heart on the part of his own people and their leaders. He had to face the fact that the leaders of Israel were irrevocably committed to opposition and would stop at nothing to destroy him. But Jesus would have known also that there was some precedent for this in the Scriptures of his own people; the archetypal servant of God described in Isaiah 53:

> was despised and rejected by men, a man of
> sorrows, and familiar with suffering.
> Like one from whom men hide their faces he
> was despised, and we esteemed him not.
> Surely he took up our infirmities and carried
> our sorrows, yet we considered him stricken
> by God, smitten by him and afflicted.
> But he was pierced for our transgressions, he
> was crushed for our iniquities; the punishment

that brought us peace was upon him, and by his
wounds we are healed.
We all, like sheep, have gone astray, each of
us has turned to his own way; and the Lord
has laid on him the iniquity of us all.
He was oppressed and afflicted, yet he did
not open his mouth;
He was led like a lamb to the slaughter, and
as a sheep before her shearers is silent, so
he did not open his mouth.
By oppression and judgment, he was taken away.
And who can speak of his descendants?
For he was cut off from the land of the living;
for the transgression of my people he was stricken.
He was assigned a grave with the wicked, and
with the rich in his death, though he had done no
violence, nor was any deceit in his mouth.
Yet it was the Lord's will to crush him and cause
him to suffer, and though the Lord makes his life
a guilt offering, he will see his offspring and
prolong his days, and the will of the Lord will
prosper in his hand.
After the suffering of his soul, he will see
the light of life and be satisfied; by his
knowledge my righteous servant will justify
many, and he will bear their iniquities. (Isa. 53:3–11)

On such slender clues here and elsewhere in the sacred
Scriptures rested Jesus's understanding of his mission and his
fate. He did not seek martyrdom and had, indeed, studiously
avoided, as far as possible, confrontation with both the
secular and the religious authorities. To the very last he
prayed that this cup should pass from him. For one dreadful
moment towards the end of his ordeal on the cross he
shuddered at the thought that he might have been mistaken.
But he would live again to see the travail of his soul and to be
satisfied, and to be united with those faulty but faithful
disciples who at that point were the sole representatives of his
Kingdom on earth.

10

AN ENCOUNTER WITH GOD

[Mark 9:2–32]

[2]After six days Jesus took Peter, James and John with him and led them up a high mountain, where they were all alone. There he was transfigured before them. [3]His clothes became dazzling white, whiter than anyone in the world could bleach them. [4]And there appeared before them Elijah and Moses, who were talking with Jesus.

[5]Peter said to Jesus, "Rabbi, it is good for us to be here. Let us put up three shelters—one for you, one for Moses and one for Elijah." [6](He did not know what to say, they were so frightened.)

[7]Then a cloud appeared and enveloped them, and a voice came from the cloud: "This is my Son, whom I love. Listen to him!"

[8]Suddenly, when they looked round, they no longer saw anyone with them except Jesus.

[9]As they were coming down the mountain, Jesus gave them orders not to tell anyone what they had seen until the Son of Man had risen from the dead. [10]They kept the matter to themselves, discussing what "rising from the dead" meant.

[11]And they asked him, "Why do the teachers of the law say that Elijah must come first?"

[12]Jesus replied, "To be sure, Elijah does come first, and restores all things. Why then is it written that the Son of Man must suffer much and be rejected? [13]But I tell you, Elijah has come, and they have done to him everything they wished, just as it is written about him."

[14]When they came to the other disciples, they saw a large crowd around them and the teachers of the law arguing with them. [15]As soon as all the people saw Jesus, they were overwhelmed with wonder and ran to greet him.

[16]"What are you arguing with them about?" he asked.

[17]A man in the crowd answered, "Teacher, I brought you my son, who is possessed by a spirit that has robbed him of speech. [18]Whenever

it seizes him, it throws him to the ground. He foams at the mouth, gnashes his teeth and becomes rigid. I asked your disciples to drive out the spirit, but they could not."

[19]"O unbelieving generation," Jesus replied, "how long shall I stay with you? How long shall I put up with you? Bring the boy to me."

[20]So they brought him. When the spirit saw Jesus, it immediately threw the boy into a convulsion. He fell to the ground and rolled around, foaming at the mouth.

[21]Jesus asked the boy's father, "How long has he been like this?"

"From childhood," he answered. [22]"It has often thrown him into fire or water to kill him. But if you can do anything, take pity on us and help us."

[23]"'If you can'?" said Jesus. "Everything is possible for him who believes."

[24]Immediately the boy's father exclaimed, "I do believe; help me overcome my unbelief!"

[25]When Jesus saw that a crowd was running to the scene, he rebuked the evil spirit. "You deaf and mute spirit," he said, "I command you, come out of him and never enter him again."

[26]The spirit shrieked, convulsed him violently and came out. The boy looked so much like a corpse that many said, "He's dead." [27]But Jesus took him by the hand and lifted him to his feet, and he stood up.

[28]After Jesus had gone indoors, his disciples asked him privately, "Why couldn't we drive it out?"

[29]He replied, "This kind can come out only by prayer."

[30]They left that place and passed through Galilee. Jesus did not want anyone to know where they were, [31]because he was teaching his disciples. He said to them, "The Son of Man is going to be betrayed into the hands of men. They will kill him, and after three days he will rise." [32]But they did not understand what he meant and were afraid to ask him about it.

The passage stands apart from all the others considered in this book. It is about an experience of God which we may expect to defy description and to mock at explanation. It offers a view from a mountain peak, looking back to Jesus's baptism and the beginning of his ministry, and looking forward to his death and resurrection which marked the end of his ministry.

But true to the genius of his race, Mark preserves a few homely touches which would normally be considered out of place in a transcendent experience of this kind. Oddly, it would seem to us, he concentrates not on the person of Jesus but on the clothes he was wearing, and is struck by the homely comparison with the best that a fuller (or bleacher) could do. He retains the normal title which the disciples used of Jesus on earth, i.e. 'Rabbi', whereas Matthew and Luke substitute for it reverential terms more suitable for the occasion. And then he exhibits Peter as a man so overcome by it all that, feeling that he has to say something, he says something wholly inconsequential.

It is interesting to observe that Matthew tones the language down a little out of regard for the chief of the apostles. But if Peter was Mark's informant, Mark has conveyed accurately the intense dismay and alarm which the apostles must have felt. There are other minor variations that the reader may see for himself (Matt. 17:1–8; Luke 9:28–36). Matthew and Luke add to the words which were heard from the cloud, without any significant extension of meaning, and more significantly Luke vouchsafes the information that Jesus had gone up into the mountain to pray, and that it was as he was praying that his countenance was altered.

All the synoptists agree that the Transfiguration took place on a mountain, that the voice was heard from a cloud, that Moses and Elijah were present, that the disciples were afraid, and that in accordance with Jesus's instructions they kept silent about the incident until after the resurrection. In all three gospels the event plays a dominant part in the narrative, signalling the end of the Galilean ministry to the general public, and the beginning of a long period of instruction for the disciples, which occupied most of the journey from the mountain to Jerusalem.

Hermon

'From the mountain'. No indication is given by the evangelist as to which mountain it was. There are many mountains to choose from in northern Israel: the only clue given by Mark and Matthew is that it was a 'high' mountain. It is an old tradition, popularised by Jerome in the fourth century, that the mountain was Tabor, ten miles south-west of the Sea of Galilee. This is indeed the site which now appears on the tourist itinerary, understandably because it is at a convenient distance from other biblical sites and readily approached by road.

But no early reader of St Mark's gospel who was familiar with the Holy Land would naturally have thought of Tabor – and for two reasons. First, in the passage quoted above it is said that Jesus left that place and passed through Galilee; then in a subsequent verse (Mark 9:33) that they came to Capernaum, but a glance at a map will show what a strange route this would have been. Given the vagueness of place names in Mark's gospel this would not be conclusive evidence. But the second objection is that Mark does insist that it was a *high* mountain. Tabor is a mere 1,800 ft above sea-level – a 'high' mountain only to those accustomed to the fens or to the countryside of Lincolnshire.

To those who lived in Palestine the phrase would more likely have suggested Mount Hermon, twelve miles north-east of Caesarea Philippi, rising to a height of over nine thousand feet. Snow-covered for most of the year, this is the high mountain most of the inhabitants would be aware of, visible from almost everywhere in the land, dominating the scenery. It has the advantage, too, of being the nearest to the place of the previously recorded incident at Caesarea Philippi. Tabor would have had a Roman fortress on top of it in the time of Jesus, and would hardly have provided the solitude for which he was clearly looking.

Hermon is part of a range offering a variety of places where Jesus and his disciples could be on their own, without requiring that they should climb to one of the three peaks. We must not suppose that Hermon was a kind of Everest, accessible only to skilled and athletic mountaineers. It did not represent what we might call now a 'challenge to the human spirit', but a prominent place on the landscape, impressive enough to be associated with the habitation of God himself. The name 'Hermon' means 'belonging to, or connected with a sanctuary'. It was a site for worship way back in Old Testament times, and the ruins of Roman temples have been discovered on the lower slopes of the mountain.

So the Transfiguration was not something which just happened to a group of people on a country walk. It has to be assumed that Jesus went there from nearby Caesarea Philippi not just in search of solitude, but in the knowledge that it was a place associated with the manifestation of God. A mountain was long regarded as the dwelling-place of God, whether it be Sinai, Carmel or Hermon, long before it came to be regarded in modern times as a 'challenge to the human spirit'. What was significant on this occasion was that it was the God of Israel who appeared there, 'the high and lofty one who inhabits eternity', and he appears in company with two men of Israel who had been regarded beyond any shadow of doubt as his true representatives on earth. The Transfiguration is an encounter with God not dissimilar to that associated with the giving of the Law at Sinai and the victory over false gods at Carmel.

What really happened

The question which presses upon the modern reader is not so much where and when the Transfiguration took place, but *if* it took place at all. We might put the question this way. Would accompanying cameramen, photographers and reporters have brought anything back to the subeditor if they had been there? Did something happen which could have been reported in *The Times* or the *Mirror*? Would we have been offered on the nine o'clock news a series of shots accompanied by an excited commentary on the dramatic and stunning activity on the lower slopes of Hermon? But that, of course, is only a serious question if we regard as true only those events which can be described and photographed, or if we insist that the only events are those which happen in the full glare of publicity.

It must be obvious to most readers, as it is to me, that some of the most important things that happen to us are those that happen within, out of sight, without perceptible consequences, and with no permanent record outside the private diary of the person concerned. I have, for example, for the greater part of my career, been involved in public life and I even dared to think occasionally that I was actually moulding public events, however humbly. My name appeared in the papers from time to time, and I figured occasionally in the news bulletins. But I know that this outward life, which seems to dominate us most of the time, was nothing like as important as events, perceptions and impressions in my inner life which shaped and controlled my feelings and attitudes, my hopes and fears, my shames and my gratifications.

The Hebrew mind at its best would never have surrendered to a view of life which exalted the seen above the unseen, or the outward above the inward. When Mark recorded this incident he recorded what he took to be the crucial event in the life of Peter, James and John, and of Jesus himself. It would never have occurred to him to ask the questions which we habitually ask. History for him was the outward expression of the activity of God in the human soul and beneath the flux of outward events. For a moment on Hermon the veil is drawn apart and the ceaseless activity of God is revealed in the conversation with Moses and Elijah and in the voice from heaven.

Visions

In the New Testament generally, visions were regarded as events, and were carefully distinguished from dream or hallucination. Strangely enough, it is Luke, a Gentile, who makes the point most clearly. He says that 'Peter and his companions were very sleepy, but when they were fully awake, they saw his glory and the two men that stood with him' (Luke 9:32). Peter thought he was dreaming when, in Acts 12, he was delivered from prison by an angel, but when Peter was come to himself he said: 'Now I know without a doubt that the Lord sent his angel and rescued me from Herod's clutches' (Acts 12:11). Luke records that when the light shone round about Paul on the road to Damascus: 'The men travelling with Saul stood there speechless; they heard the sound but did not see anyone' (Acts 9:7).

These visions were real events. The Transfiguration determined the course of Jesus's ministry until the end of his time on earth. Peter, delivered from prison, conducted a long and effective mission. Paul was converted, and subsequently engaged on a course which was to change the history of Europe. Experiences of vision in the New Testament are more than matched by the experiences recorded in the Old Testament.

The Lord appeared to Abraham and he became the founder of a nation (Gen. 17:1–2). He appeared to Jacob and he founded a dynasty (Gen. 35:11). He appeared to Moses in the burning bush (Exod. 3:2) and Moses became a vehicle of the Law which has dominated society in the west ever since. He appeared to Samuel, and the monarchy was born (1 Sam. 3). He appeared to Amos, Hosea, Isaiah and Jeremiah with profound consequences for Israel and for the whole world. Vision was in the Hebrew mind an instrument of beneficent change, the means by which the Lord of all the earth caused his will to be done.

I am not suggesting, of course, that vision of this kind is confined to the Hebrew people or to the Christian Church. Nevertheless, the Hebrew attitude towards vision does have certain distinctive features. There is no suggestion anywhere within the pages of Scripture that vision was something to be sought or to be pursued for its own sake. Vision was not regarded as a blessing or as a sign of approval by those who received it. The usual reaction was dismay and fear and a reluctance to take it seriously. Vision was by no means always associated with spectacular events. The burning bush which Moses turned aside to see was not a wholly unprecedented event as modern horticulturalists will tell us. It caught the attention, no more. The young Samuel simply heard a voice, and was at a loss to explain it. Jeremiah's was no beatific vision, but the sight of an almond tree in bloom.

I shall not weary the reader with any more examples of the obvious. The great thing in the Hebrew mind was that it led to action and change, usually at great cost to the person involved. The history of the Hebrews is inexplicable if we do not take seriously their own evaluation of it; it was a history initiated and controlled by God and at special points in it illuminated by the vision of him.

The history of Jesus defies understanding if we are not prepared to believe that he was supremely aware of God's will and God's presence, and from time to time (and not just at the Baptism or at the Transfiguration) was sustained by the vision of his Father in heaven. Once we allow for the possibility that something happened on the mountain, more or less along the lines described by Mark, then we have to go on to ask the question: What did it mean? What did it mean to Mark and the Church for which he wrote? What did it mean to the disciples who shared in the experience? What did it mean to Jesus himself?

What it meant to the early Church

Jesus had said, apparently, that some of his companions would not taste death before they had seen the Kingdom of God come with power (Mark 9:1; John 21:22–3). As the first disciples grew older and some had already been martyred, expectation in some parts of the Church reached fever pitch, and it was to this problem that Paul addressed himself when he wrote his second letter to the Thessalonians: 'Concerning the coming of our Lord Jesus Christ and our being gathered to him, we ask you, brothers, not to become easily unsettled or alarmed by some prophecy, report or letter supposed to have come from us, saying that the day of the Lord has already come' (2 Thess. 2:1–2).

The nature and timing of Jesus's return as prophesied by Holy Scripture has been, and remains, a divisive issue in the Church. Mark would have been aware of it in his own time and in his own congregation. He may be suggesting therefore that the Transfiguration was, in part at least, a fulfilment of the words, 'I tell you the truth, some who are standing here will not taste death before they see the Kingdom of God come with power'. We cannot be certain on that issue, but I think we can be certain that there is a connection in his mind between the Transfiguration and the ultimate return in glory.

Another issue which troubled the early Church was concerned with the relationship of the Christian believers to their Jewish predecessors. They were bound to ask why it was that the Jewish people, generally, had rejected their own Messiah. If his own people had not believed in him why should anyone else believe in him? The story of the Transfiguration did provide some answer to this question. The official leaders of Judaism had been consistently hostile to Jesus's mission, as we have already seen, and they were to prove their hostility by Jesus's subsequent arrest and crucifixion. They of course did not know about the Transfiguration. They had often asked for a 'sign from heaven', but were never granted one because any faith which depends upon dramatic signs from heaven is unlikely to be genuine or lasting.

It is significant that it was only the inner circle of the disciples who shared in the experience. Peter had just avowed his faith in Jesus as the Messiah and now he and his companions could safely be given a reassuring 'sign from heaven'. But this sign from heaven included a conversation with Moses and Elijah. Moses and Elijah were there in their representative capacity, Moses standing for the Law of Israel, and Elijah standing for the prophets. The point is that while the present leaders of Israel dismissed Jesus as an imposter, the real leaders of Israel – Moses and the prophets – were shown to be on his side. The Jews were being summoned to 'hear' Jesus as they had previously claimed to be hearing Moses and Elijah.

This was an important message for the Church because it suggested that Gentile believers were in the true succession to the faithful Israelites of old, and could regard themselves as inheritors of a tradition previously confined to the Jews. The little Christian assembly on a street corner in Rome was not just another new sect with which the ancient world abounded, but a body of people sharing a long history, back to Abraham himself, inheritors of the great promise which the Jewish leaders of their day had spurned. Thus for Mark, and for his readers, the Transfiguration would have been loaded with meaning not only for their faith in Christ but for their relationships with the old Israel. The Church could rightly call itself the New Israel, inheriting the ancient promises and hearing the voice which spoke not from Sinai but from Hermon. The problem which Paul faced everywhere in his mission was potentially resolved for those who had eyes to see the meaning of what happened that day on the mountain of Transfiguration.

What did it mean to the disciples?

The second question is, what did it mean to the three disciples who were present? They had had a long and harrowing experience, as the result of their call to discipleship three years earlier. It had been an exciting but at times unnerving experience, as with their master they had become the target of official opposition. Moreover, their relationship with Jesus had not always been as easy as they might have wished; they had come in for their own share of criticism for failing to understand the mission to which Jesus was committed. Their vision of the long-promised Kingdom in which Jesus would be King and they would be sharing in the honours had been seriously disturbed by the solemn warnings of the cost of their own discipleship. They had struggled through to a kind of faith in him which had been articulated by Peter at Caesarea Philippi, but it had been a hard battle, and their faith remained precarious.

There is no suggestion in the gospel that Jesus knew what was going to happen when he climbed the slopes of Hermon. He, and the three disciples closest to him, had often withdrawn from the public scene for refreshment and rest; but what happened on the mountain proved to be not only the confirmation of what Peter had previously professed, but the vindication of their own long and painful commitment to him. Of course, their doubts were never wholly put to rest, and the event that lay ahead taxed their faith to the uttermost. They would all desert Jesus at the time of trial. Peter would deny him, and Judas betray him. But at least they could look back through the mists of their own failure and the disasters of Holy Week and Good Friday in the knowledge that they had seen the Lord transfigured on the mountain (2 Pet. 1:18).

They were far from understanding the relationship between Jesus and the God of their fathers, as indeed the Church today is still far from understanding it, but they could no longer doubt that their master did indeed enjoy a relationship with God unprecedented in the history of their people. With Moses and Elijah standing by, they had listened to the words 'Hear him'. There were to be many occasions on which, both before and after the resurrection, they failed to hear him; but at least they knew that, when they did hear him, they were hearing the voice of God himself. So it was the Transfiguration, perhaps more than any other single event, which gave them the courage to endure and to survive all that lay ahead.

What did it mean to Jesus?

The third question is one we hardly dare to ask and certainly cannot command an answer: What did it mean to Jesus himself? He was no ordinary man, and he could hardly be unconscious of something special in his relationship with God even as compared with the great saints of old, Abraham, Moses and the prophets. But nevertheless he was an ordinary man, who ate and slept, walked and talked like any other man. He would hardly have been man at all if he had not known doubts and fears and uncertainties. What made him different was that he invariably transcended them in his pure desire to do the will of God. He did not need special gifts of foresight, however, to know that he had aroused the implacable opposition of the leaders of Israel, and they would 'get him' in the end.

Therefore his coming visit to Jerusalem for the Passover could be a time of deadly peril, both for him and for his followers. In Philip the tetrarch's territory he was reasonably safe; in Jerusalem he would be naked to his enemies – and they would have no mercy. He had climbed the mountain, responding to a dim instinct in his own heart that something important was about to happen. His 'retreat' was overtaken by an ineffable experience of the living God, combined with a solemn warning of what lay ahead. This conviction may well lie behind Luke's account of the narrative when he suggests that Moses and Elijah talked to Jesus about his coming 'exodus' at Jerusalem (the exact Greek word for exodus is used here).

From this point onwards Jesus is always en route for Jerusalem and takes the opportunity of reminding the disciples again and again of what lay ahead of them there. From the heights of Hermon in glory he had discerned the outlines of that little hill outside Jerusalem on which he was to die a shameful death. Hermon and Calvary must be held together in Christian theology – the glory and the shame, the rapture and the pain, the vision and the darkness.

The Transfiguration was an essential element in Jesus's understanding of himself and of his mission. It is for this reason, perhaps, that the incident stands at the heart of Mark's gospel, interpreting the past and delineating the future. It serves to emphasise the point, made earlier in this chapter, that vision is not a reward for a godly life but a preparation for the rigors and the tragedies ahead. It is an important lesson for the Christian disciple, sometimes painfully aware of the apparent contrast between the early exciting days of his discipleship, marked by enthusiasm and vision, and the latter days when 'the sun and the light and the moon and the stars grow dark, and the clouds return after the rain, when the keepers of the house tremble and the strong men stoop' (Eccles. 12:2–3).

This is not necessarily a sign of declining faith or unconscious apostasy. The vision we have at the beginning is not a sign of virtue or a mark of achievement; it is a gracious gift, intended to help the pilgrim tread the sometimes dolorous path which lies ahead of him or her. The vision contains no promise of a comfortable life or easy victories. That is why all the great men of God before and after Christ echo Isaiah in response to his vision in the Temple: 'Woe is me . . . my eyes have seen the King, the Lord Almighty' (Isa. 6:5). He that comes to the Lord, let him prepare his soul for temptation.

11

THE RICH MAN

[Mark 10:13–31]

[13] People were bringing little children to Jesus to have him touch them, but the disciples rebuked them. [14] When Jesus saw this, he was indignant. He said to them, "Let the little children come to me, and do not hinder them, for the kingdom of God belongs to such as these. [15] I tell you the truth, anyone who will not receive the kingdom of God like a little child will never enter it."

[16] And he took the children in his arms, put his hands on them and blessed them.

[17] As Jesus started on his way, a man ran up to him and fell on his knees before him. "Good teacher," he asked, "what must I do to inherit eternal life?"

[18] "Why do you call me good?" Jesus answered. "No-one is good —except God alone. [19] You know the commandments: 'Do not murder, do not commit adultery, do not steal, do not give false testimony, do not defraud, honour your father and mother.'"

[20] "Teacher," he declared, "all these I have kept since I was a boy."

[21] Jesus looked at him and loved him. "One thing you lack," he said. "Go, sell everything you have and give to the poor, and you will have treasure in heaven. Then come, follow me."

[22] At this the man's face fell. He went away sad, because he had great wealth.

[23] Jesus looked around and said to his disciples, "How hard it is for the rich to enter the kingdom of God!"

[24] The disciples were amazed at his words. But Jesus said again, "Children, how hard it is to enter the kingdom of God! [25] It is easier for a camel to go through the eye of a needle than for a rich man to enter the kingdom of God."

[26] The disciples were even more amazed, and said to each other, "Who then can be saved?"

[27]Jesus looked at them and said, "With man this is impossible, but not with God; all things are possible with God."

[28]Peter said to him, "We have left everything to follow you!"

[29]"I tell you the truth," Jesus replied, "no-one who has left home or brothers or sisters or mother or father or children or fields for me and the gospel [30]will fail to receive a hundred times as much in this present age (homes, brothers, sisters, mothers, children and fields—and with them, persecutions) and in the age to come, eternal life. [31]But many who are first will be last, and the last first."

This section has all the appearance of an artless and straightforward narrative, but it raises issues which we need to be aware of. I mention a few of them. The story of the rich man is not confined to what we call the canonical gospels, that is to say, those gospels which have been from the earliest times part of the New Testament. Our present New Testament was achieved by a process of selection, or, more properly, deselection, and there are many so-called 'gospels' which purport to give us information which is not included in the New Testament. They often use the name of an apostle to give them a certain prestige, for example, the Gospel of Thomas, the Gospel of Peter, the Gospel of Nicodemus, the Gospel of Philip, the Gospel of Mary. There is, too, a so-called 'Gospel of the Hebrews', which bears some similarity to Matthew's gospel, and here is the story of the rich man as it appears in it:

The rich man said to him, 'Master, what good thing shall I do in order to have life?' He said to him, 'Man, keep the Law and the Prophets.' 'I have kept them,' was his reply. He said to him, 'Go, sell all that you possess and share it out among the poor, and come follow me.' Then the rich man began to scratch his head; he did not like it. The Lord said to him, 'Now can you say I have kept the Law and the Prophets? It is written in the Law thou shalt love thy neighbour as thyself, and look, many of your brothers, sons of Abraham, are dressed in filthy rags and dying of hunger while your house is full of many good things, yet nothing at all goes forth from it to them.' Then he turned and said to his disciple Simon, who was sitting beside him, 'Simon, son of John, it is easier for a camel to enter in through a needle's eye than for a rich man to enter the Kingdom of Heaven.'

The apocryphal gospels were fragmentary and later than the canonical gospels. They seldom add anything essential to our knowledge of Christ, but, as we shall see later, they may help in questions of detail.

Variations in the text

The gospels we now have in front of us are the end-product of a long process of 'transmission'; they have been copied and recopied down the ages since their production, on the whole as far as we can tell with remarkably few deviations from the original text. But in such a long process there have been errors or misunderstandings, or well-intentioned attempts to improve the meaning. So in this passage the manuscripts to which we have access vary from each other, and it is a matter of technical skill to choose between them.

There are variations in the order of the commandments quoted, presumably according to the version of the Ten Commandments familiar to the scribe or copyist. In some manuscripts the commandment 'Do not defraud' is omitted altogether because it is not part of the original decalogue. These variations, you will see, are of little importance except to the textual scholar. But others do raise more serious questions.

For example, in the margin of the NIV there is a footnote to the effect that some manuscripts amend verse 24 to read, 'How hard it is for those who trust in riches to enter the kingdom of God.' This would be regarded by most scholars as an amendment designed to soften the impact of the words on those in the early Church who found them too uncompromising in their condemnation of wealth. That is why in the NIV they are consigned to a footnote.

The word for camel was replaced in some of the early versions by a word which means rope, presumably because the scribe concerned thought that the illustration was altogether too absurd. But of course the whole point of the illustration was that it was absurd and was intended to amuse.

Recent researches have uncovered the fact that it did have some currency in the ancient world as an example of the impossible.

Variations between the gospels

In addition to variations within the text of a gospel, there are variations between the gospels. Among several examples in this passage I take two by way of illustration. In Mark, which I am presuming is the earliest of the three synoptic gospels, nothing is said about the man whom Jesus encountered on the road except that he 'had great wealth'. Matthew, on the other hand, perhaps misled by verse 20, says that he was a *young* man. Luke says that he was a 'ruler', wishing perhaps to make the point that there were certain well-respected men in the Jewish community who, for all their devotion to the Law, felt that there was something missing with the Judaism of their day. This would have been an important point to make in the early Church, given the growing conflict between Jews and Christians.

The second illustration is more far-reaching in its implications for Christian doctrine. Mark quotes Jesus as saying 'Why do you call me good? . . . No-one is good except God alone' (Mark 10:18). Matthew is concerned that it might be misunderstood in a Church where already disputes were beginning to arise concerning the exact nature of Jesus and his relationship to God. Was Jesus suggesting that he was not good? So in a rather clumsy alteration Matthew substitutes for Mark's question: 'Why do you ask me about what is good?' (Matt. 19:17). The textual scholar trying to establish the original utterance would undoubtedly prefer the Marcan to the Matthean rendering as being the more primitive of the two.

The reader may be forgiven for thinking that these are rather pettifogging distinctions without any significance for the contemporary Christian struggling to bring up a family, coping with illness or looking for a job. But for the serious student of the New Testament they are important insofar as they open a door on to the social and intellectual environment in which Jesus lived and the gospels were written.

The Marcan Outline

The issue to which I now turn will more readily be seen to be of great importance to our understanding of the life and ministry of Jesus. Matthew, on the whole, follows the Marcan order in the narrative which covers the period from the Transfiguration to the entry into Jerusalem. He makes certain additions to the narrative, but he does not substantially alter it. In Luke's gospel, on the other hand, the Marcan order virtually disappears. In its place we have what is called 'a travel document' which describes a long journey from Caesarea Philippi to Jerusalem and includes a whole series of incidents, parables and sayings which Luke has at his disposal, but which he cannot fit into the Marcan framework (Luke 9:51–18:34).

Some of the most valuable and familiar gospel material is thus made available to us, but it certainly distorts, and to some extent obscures, the distinctive message which Mark is at pains to convey. Perhaps this is the point, therefore, to say something about the 'Marcan outline'. In everyday life even a trivial incident derives most of its significance from the circumstances under which it occurred. A scratch on the side of the car is an everyday occurrence, but it will be in the Sunday newspapers if it is the result of a collision between the Sovereign's limousine and the car of a foreign embassy in London. We cannot begin to understand an incident in the gospel if we do not know about the people involved in it or the circumstances under which it occurred.

Already, I trust, an outline has begun to emerge from Mark's gospel. Most of chapter 1, like the early part of John's gospel, is a kind of prologue. There follows a section describing the enthusiastic reaction of ordinary people to Jesus's ministry in Galilee. Then, as we have seen, opposition to him begins to mount and he is virtually a fugitive, moving from one location to another to avoid arrest. At the point of maximum tension Jesus evokes a crucial confession of faith from his disciples which is confirmed by the experience on the Mount cf Transfiguration. From this point until the entry into Jerusalem the narrative is dominated by two words which reveal Mark's intention.

The first is the word 'disciple'. Disciples are mentioned severally or together no less than nine times in this part of Mark's narrative. The second word is 'the way' which appears six times. Of course it is possible to say that any journey is bound to contain references to the way: that is not the point. The combination of the word 'disciples' and the word for 'the way' makes it clear that Mark intends us to understand this period between the Transfiguration and the entry into Jerusalem as a period dominated by the instruction of the disciples. They are to be instructed in 'the way', and it is no accident that the early Christians were called 'people of the way'.

But Mark is not concerned just with what happened thirty or forty years ago in Palestine; he wishes the reader to understand that the true disciple has to make his own spiritual journey from the moment of his illumination and conversion to the inevitable confrontation with the world and the powers of darkness. Like the first disciples he has to pass from Hermon to Jerusalem. This is the significance of the verses immediately after the Transfiguration: 'Jesus did not want anyone to know where they were because he was teaching his disciples. He said to them, "The Son of Man is going to be betrayed into the hands of men. They will kill him and after three days he will rise"' (Mark 9:30–1). More alarming still was his warning to the disciples that they would be called to deny themselves and to take up their cross (Mark 8:34).

This was the situation in the troubled times in which Mark and his fellow believers lived. There were indeed Christians 'taking up their cross', being harassed and persecuted and sometimes executed for their faith. The cross was not for them an object of pious veneration; it was an ever-present threat in a cruel world dominated by quixotic emperors and paid informers. The context therefore is all-important to our understanding of Mark's intention. Luke may well have understood that intention, but his treatment of Jesus's last journey to Jerusalem certainly obscures it.

Children and Disciples

The reader will be relieved to know that at least on one point all three synoptic evangelists are agreed. They wish us to understand that there is a connection between the blessing of the children and the encounter with the rich man. The rich man, by his own admission, had made an honest, if laboured, attempt to fulfil the commands of the Law, and Jesus honours him for it. Mark even goes so far as to say that he loved him, or as we might say 'took to him', in his frank confession of failure.

For all the effort of a lifetime there was still something missing. He was no more sure of inheriting eternal life than when he began. Mark probably intended us to see the rich man as a symbol of the Jewish people as a whole, so diligent in their observance of the Law, so self-denying in their obedience to its commands, so deadly serious about the issues of life, and so disciplined in their pursuit of the Kingdom as they understood it. For many worthy souls in Israel it was toil, sweat and tears all the way, with apparently little to show for it at the end. They tried hard but missed the point.

The children, on the other hand, were not trying at all; they were young and innocent and unaffected, fresh and optimistic. Jesus saw in them a type of the ideal disciple, trusting in the Lord, confident in the future, ready for a blessing. Such were Jesus's own disciples. They were not seeking some far-off objective; they were not like Saul of Tarsus, burdened with the demands of the Law or stricken in conscience as a result of failing to keep it. They were not rich or powerful or clever. They were just children – enthusiastic, confident (overconfident, we might say) but devoted to Christ and eager to be in his presence. They had, indeed, as Peter said, given up everything to follow him – their boats, their nets, their assured income, their home delights. They were not locked into the world as the rich man was. When the moment of choice came to them they did not sorrowfully go away.

Wealth

The scribe who qualified the seemingly harsh utterance of verse 24 to make it more palatable to the community in which he lived, has done us a service, even if he has been relegated to a footnote. The problem to which he alerts us is one which was familiar to the early Church and has remained so ever since. The same issue arises in the beatitudes where Luke says bluntly, 'Blessed are you poor', and Matthew seems to qualify the utterance by saying, 'Blessed are the poor in spirit'. It is difficult for a rich man to enter the Kingdom of God because whether he wishes it or not he comes to trust in his riches as a hedge against accident and disaster. In that sense, if in that sense alone, the unknown scribe was right – no man can at the same time wholly trust in God and still permit himself to trust in his riches.

But the Christian Church never developed a thoroughly rigorist attitude to wealth. Ananias and Sapphira did not incur their fearful penalty because they had kept back part of the proceeds of the sale of their land, but because they pretended that they were whole-hearted in their sacrifice of material goods, when in fact they were keeping part of it back as an insurance against a rainy day (Acts 5). Barnabas, on the other hand, who was a wealthy man, did not prevaricate. He sold his field and handed over the whole proceeds to the Church.

The attitude of the early Church was severely practical; rich men were expected to contribute to the needs of poor men, rich churches, as the collection by St Paul makes clear, were expected to support the churches which were less well-endowed. The rich man of the gospel was not being asked to pursue poverty as a way to perfection but, more simply, to sell everything he had and give it to the poor. In that sense the writer of the gospel of the Hebrews had it right. How could he say that he kept the Law when his 'brothers, Sons of

Abraham, were dressed in filthy rags and dying of hunger while his house was full of many good things'? It is not poverty for its own sake that is the Christian ideal, but openness of hand and generosity of spirit.

Eternal Life

The rich man came asking for the secret of 'eternal life' which for all his devotion to the Law he had not found. He was hedged about with the signs of his own mortality, fearful of what the next day might bring, increasingly aware of the ambiguities of his own existence, haunted by the frailty of life and the transitoriness of all human achievement. He is a lucky man who is never haunted by such considerations. Lucky? But it is precisely this painful awareness of the limitations of human life that causes people to seek 'eternal life', not in the sense of unlimited extension of our conditions here on earth but in the sense of a new dimension of life which imparts some sense of significance to the here and now.

Poets and prophets of the Old Testament express themselves frequently on this subject and never more powerfully than in these haunting words from Isaiah 40:6–8: 'All men are like grass, and all their glory is like the flowers of the field. The grass withers and the flowers fall, because the breath of the Lord blows on them. Surely the people are grass. The grass withers and the flowers fall.' Or this from Psalm 39: 'Man walks in a vain shadow and disquiets himself in vain. He heaps up riches and cannot tell who shall gather them'. Or these words, frequently used at the funeral service – 'We brought nothing into this world, and it is certain we can carry nothing out' (Job 1:21).

But, for the Hebrew mind, the melancholy sense of the transitoriness of life only served to enhance their sense of the permanence and eternity of God. 'Before the mountains were born or you brought forth the earth and the world, from everlasting to everlasting you are God' (Ps. 90:2). So, in their view, the characteristic features of life on earth, our weakness, our mortality, are the means by which we reach out to one who is eternal in the heavens. It is the very nature of man that he should cease; it is the very nature of God that he should be for ever.

When the rich man came asking for eternal life he was expressing the longing, not only of his own people, but of the whole human race, for a relationship with the eternal God whose gift it was to impart eternal life to mortal men. It is noticeable that Jesus did not promise him eternal life. In the vocabulary of the day that might well have been misunderstood, but he did promise him treasure in heaven, and it was this treasure which, for the moment at least, the rich man forfeited out of devotion to his treasure on earth.

The First and the Last

As if there were not complications enough, there is one more to be considered in the last verse of the passage: 'Many who are first shall be last, and the last first'. If the context is important in determining the meaning of any one incident in the gospels, the context is almost indispensable in determining the meaning of an utterance such as this. It does not appear in all the Marcan manuscripts. It is omitted at this point by Luke. It seems to be what is sometimes called 'a floating logion', i.e. an utterance of Jesus which may have been repeated on various occasions, or may be in the tradition which the evangelist received, but which could not be accurately located in any one part of the gospel. Matthew quotes it twice, here and at 20:16, after the parable of the labourers in the vineyard. Luke omits it here, but quotes it after the parable of the narrow door (Luke 13:30).

Great ingenuity has been exercised determining what its meaning is in its present Marcan context. It has been suggested, for example, that it is a hidden reference to the life and ministry of St Paul, who came last in the order of the apostolate, but in Mark's view came first in order of achievement for the Kingdom. If it is closely tied to the present passage it could be a warning to the disciples that although they were first in the field as disciples, even the rich man who for the moment had turned away might ultimately take his place in the Kingdom before them.

Or it could be yet another reference to the well-worn issue of the relationship between the Jews and the Christians. The Jews had without doubt been first as the chosen people of God, but because of their opposition to Jesus they had forfeited their place and the others were pressing in ahead of them. There is no way of knowing which interpretation is right. It could be that like many another public speaker Jesus often quoted the words, but with a variety of meanings and applications. Whatever else it may mean it is certainly a reminder that there are some strange reversals of fortune in the human experience. It is true that some highly successful people turn out in the end to have failed, and some inconspicuous man, thought unworthy of attention, ultimately triumphs. 'One who puts on his armour should not boast like one who takes it off' (1 Kgs. 20:11), 'The race is not to the swift or the battle to the strong' (Eccles. 9:11).

12

BARTIMAEUS

[Mark 10:46–11:10]

[46] Then they came to Jericho. As Jesus and his disciples, together with a large crowd, were leaving the city, a blind man, Bartimaeus (that is, the Son of Timaeus), was sitting by the roadside begging. [47] When he heard that it was Jesus of Nazareth, he began to shout, "Jesus, Son of David, have mercy on me!"

[48] Many rebuked him and told him to be quiet, but he shouted all the more, "Son of David, have mercy on me!"

[49] Jesus stopped and said, "Call him."

So they called to the blind man, "Cheer up! On your feet! He's calling you." [50] Throwing his cloak aside, he jumped to his feet and came to Jesus.

[51] "What do you want me to do for you?" Jesus asked him.

The blind man said, "Rabbi, I want to see."

[52] "Go," said Jesus, "your faith has healed you." Immediately he received his sight and followed Jesus along the road.

11 As they approached Jerusalem and came to Bethphage and Bethany at the Mount of Olives, Jesus sent two of his disciples, [2] saying to them, "Go to the village ahead of you, and just as you enter it, you will find a colt tied there, which no-one has ever ridden. Untie it and bring it here. [3] If anyone asks you, 'Why are you doing this?' tell him, 'The Lord needs it and will send it back here shortly.'"

[4] They went and found a colt outside in the street, tied at a doorway. As they untied it, [5] some people standing there asked, "What are you doing, untying that colt?" [6] They answered as Jesus had told them to, and the people let them go. [7] When they brought the colt to Jesus and threw their cloaks over it, he sat on it. [8] Many people spread their cloaks on the road, while others spread branches they had cut in the fields. [9] Those who went ahead and those who followed shouted,

"Hosanna!"

"Blessed is he who comes in the name of the Lord!"

[10]"Blessed is the coming kingdom of our father David!"

"Hosanna in the highest!"

After the Transfiguration and before the encounter with the 'rich man' Jesus and his disciples went to Capernaum. It was to be his last visit to what had been his only home once he left Nazareth. After that, 'Jesus then left that place and went into the region of Judea and across the Jordan' (Mark 10:1). This is a puzzling statement because the only direct route from Galilee to Judea was via Samaria. That Jesus may occasionally have used this route is borne out by John's reference to the meeting with the woman of Samaria (John 4:7), and by Luke's account of his rejection by one of the Samaritan villages (Luke 9:51–6).

The textual evidence at this point in Mark is confused and we are left with a balance of probabilities. The most likely conclusion is that Mark intended us to understand that Jesus left Galilee, crossed the Jordan by one of the several fords available, and then took the normal pilgrim route down the east side of the Jordan. The confusion is partly caused by the fact that the area called 'across the Jordan', otherwise known as Peraea, was predominantly Jewish and was, indeed, regarded by the local inhabitants as part of Judea, even though politically it belonged to Galilee and was ruled by Herod Antipas.

Peraea

Peraea was an area bounded on the west by the Jordan valley and on the east by the desert. It was rich agricultural land for the most part, which over the centuries had proved a mixed blessing because it had regularly attracted marauding tribes from the desert. But now, relatively secure under Roman rule, it provided an important trade route from Damascus to Eilat and the Red Sea. This road, sometimes known as 'The King's Highway' did not pass through the Jordan valley as such; it took the less swampy route through the uplands east of it.

Orthodox Jewish pilgrims, who wished to avoid Samaria, took that route and followed it as far as the ford across the Jordan at Jericho. It was a route which Jesus must have followed several times before. One such occasion is recorded in Luke 3, which describes a visit with his parents to Jerusalem for the feast of the Passover when he was 12 (Luke 2:41–52). As a Jew loyal to the tradition of his fathers and the demands of the Law he is likely to have observed the three main annual feasts in Jerusalem – the Passover and Feast of Unleavened Bread in the spring, the Feast of Weeks at the beginning of the wheat harvest, and the Feast of Booths when the harvest had been gathered. It remains a matter of dispute as to how often Jesus went to Jerusalem during the course of his ministry. The fourth gospel makes room for several visits, but it assumes that his ministry lasted for over three years.

Mark does not record any previous visit; his gospel can be reconstructed on the basis of a ministry of only one year. Nevertheless, Mark's narrative would certainly permit of a longer period and I incline to the view that the fourth gospel is right. If so, Jesus would have travelled this route earlier as a member of his own family from Nazareth, and later in company with his disciples. He would have been familiar with that upland scenery, the forests and the pastures, the rich fruit crops and the frequent gorges and mountain torrents, but this time it would have been different.

Luke, describing the beginning of this journey, says that Jesus 'resolutely set out for Jerusalem' (9:51), or, as we might say, gritted his teeth, and set out for the inevitable confrontation with the leaders of his people. Yes, indeed, he had been to Jerusalem before, and it seems that he had friends and followers there, but he knew now that he was making the journey for the last time.

He had been often enough a fugitive in Galilee, but on the whole Herod had refrained from moving against him. He had no desire to bloody his hands with another prophet, having been tricked by his wife into executing John the Baptist. In Jerusalem Jesus could not be sure of the protection of a large, enthusiastic crowd, but he could be sure of the bitter enmity of the Scribes and Pharisees and the political opposition of a vindictive high priest. He was, to be sure, the Son of Man, but he was also a son of man, vulnerable, anxious for himself and for his followers, only too vividly aware of what could lie ahead of him. He was walking into a trap through those pleasant uplands of Peraea, and the trap would close on him once he entered Jericho, where the writ of the High Priest ran, and the Roman governor would be on the alert.

The Caravan

The equivalent passage in Luke which covers this journey is sometimes called, as we have seen, 'Luke's Travel Document'. It begins at Luke 9:51 and ends in Jericho ten chapters later. It covers a wide range of events and includes some of the most famous of Jesus's parables, for example the parable of the lost sheep, of the prodigal son, of the rich man and Lazarus, and the good Samaritan. Luke makes no attempt at a consecutive narrative. He simply uses it as a vehicle for memorable events and important teaching for which he can find no space elsewhere in the Marcan framework.

In Mark, on the other hand, the story of the journey is relatively short and the incidents few. We have already discussed the encounter with the rich young man. Then there are the sayings about salt and divorce and an exposure of the ambitions of James and John, sons of Zebedee, and that is all. The journey was about a hundred miles and would not, at a brisk walking pace, have taken much more than a week. But it would be normal on such occasions to travel not alone or in small groups but as part of a large caravan to which many people would attach themselves for safety in a brigand-ridden area. There were after all rich pickings to be had of wealthy merchants trading between Damascus and Eilat.

So one has to envisage a party of hundreds rather than tens, and the caravan would travel at the rate of the slowest. There might well be in the caravan traders, pilgrims, soldiers, government officers, and there would have been old and young, healthy and sick, rich and poor. We must not therefore imagine Jesus and his disciples as a small cohesive group travelling apart. In such a caravan, groups would form en route and dissolve and reform and dissolve again (see Luke 2:44). Jesus may indeed have had not just his disciples but relatives or friends from Galilee making the journey with them.

The able-bodied men would expect to be armed for protection of the company against attack. It could well be that the disciples themselves would have carried weapons with them on their various journeys (see Luke 22:38). But Mark makes it clear that for all the noise and activity of such a caravan, the making of meals and provision for the pack animals, Jesus is primarily concerned at this crucial stage in his ministry to establish the truth in the minds of the disciples, which they had already dimly perceived, i.e. that the Messiah they had professed at Caesarea Philippi was not the Messiah of popular expectation. This was no triumphal journey to take his throne in Jerusalem but a journey into certain danger, and to almost certain death.

Three times since the confession at Caesarea Philippi, Jesus is recorded as having warned his disciples of what lay ahead – 'He then began to teach them that the Son of Man must suffer many things and be rejected by the elders, chief priests and teachers of the Law, and he must be killed and after three days rise again' (Mark 8:31, see also 9:31 and 10:32). These predictions have been compared to the tolling of a bell proclaiming the solemn inescapable event which lay just ahead. There were, of course, lighter moments, easy laughter, familiar fellowship, boisterous high spirits as the pilgrims drew near to the holy city. But for Jesus himself it was a journey shadowed by his conviction of what lay ahead of him. It was to happen again to one of the most famous of his followers:

> Compelled by the Spirit I am going to Jerusalem, not knowing what will happen to me there. I only know that in every city the Holy Spirit warns me that prison and hardships are facing me. However, I consider my life worth nothing to me, if only I may finish the race and complete the task . . . (Acts 20:22–4)

Of course Jesus could have avoided the issue. He need not have gone to Jerusalem at all; he could have reckoned that his main task was to continue the education of his disciples in Galilee and minister to those who had come to believe in him. But just as he was driven by the Spirit into the wilderness to be tempted of Satan, he is now driven by the same Spirit to Jerusalem and the final confrontation with the powers-that-be. It could not be, he had said, 'for surely no prophet can perish outside Jerusalem' (Luke 13:33). He had accepted the title which Peter had given to him – he was the Messiah, but his triumph lay the other side of dereliction, betrayal and death. It is to this theme of the 'crucified Messiah' that Mark devotes his gospel.

Jericho

This journey, so heavy with significance for Jesus, had to end sometime, and it ended at their first sight of Jericho. By the year 8,000 BC, so it is said, it was a large town surrounded by a stone wall in which was set a tower twenty-five feet high. It achieved fame in the biblical record as being the town which fell to the forces of Joshua en route for the Promised Land. Herod the Great, with typical extravagance, had greatly enlarged the town and had developed it on the grand scale, with accommodation for guests with gardens and a portico, and even a Roman-style bath. He had the satisfaction of spending his last days there, and dying in the palace he had built for himself. It would not have been Jesus's first visit to the city. He was baptised in the Jordan near by and the wilderness in which he was tempted was somewhere in the vicinity. Jericho was not a particularly distinguished city. As George Adam Smith puts it:

no great man was born in Jericho, no heroic deed was done in her, she had been called the key and the guardhouse of Judaea: she was only the pantry; she never stood a siege and her inhabitants were always running away.

So it is to this city, leaving the traders and the government officers to go their way on to Eilat, that the pilgrims come before they begin the last hot, steep climb to the hill of Zion. No great man was ever born in Jericho, no heroic deed was done in her, but on that day there passed through the city one who was to be the greatest of all men, the hero above all heroes, one who was to prove to be the saviour of the world.

Son of David

What happened in Jericho is recorded by all three evangelists. They differ from each other in detail. Luke says that the blind beggar (unnamed) met Jesus as he was on his way into Jericho. But that is presumably because Luke has to make space in his gospel for an incident which is not recorded elsewhere, viz. the encounter with Zaccheus, the tax-collector (Luke 19:1–10). Matthew agrees with Mark that it was as Jesus was leaving Jericho that the incident took place, but – rather strangely – insists that there were two blind men who were healed (both unnamed). This has been the source of many arguments, but with no assured results. Origen, one of the earliest expositors, identifies the two blind men with Israel and Judah:

> the blind men were Israel and Judah before Christ's coming; they were sitting 'by the way' being in the Law and Prophets. They were blind by not seeing the true meaning of the Law and the Prophets before the coming of Jesus into their soul.

This is an imaginative but scarcely convincing explanation. The Marcan account is to be preferred. The pilgrims enter from the north and go out through the west gate. It was a handy place for a blind beggar, who might expect pilgrims to be generous at the end of a long journey with the Holy City only twenty miles ahead. What is remarkable about him is the term he uses to address Jesus – 'Son of David'. This form of address is important to Mark because it emphasises the close relationship in his mind between the encounter with blind

Bartimaeus and the triumphal entry which followed – a connection which is somewhat obscured by conventional chapter divisions.

The Marcan account of the triumphal entry has the people shouting 'Hosanna! Blessed is he who comes in the name of the Lord! Blessed is the coming kingdom of our father David!' The connection is even more explicit in Matthew, where Jesus is acclaimed in precisely the same words as by Bartimaeus – 'Hosanna to the Son of David'. The description of Jesus as the Son of David was – in the view of the evangelists – strictly true. Joseph, Luke says, was a descendant of David (Luke 1:27). When Caesar Augustus issued a decree that a census should be taken of the entire Roman world, Joseph and Mary were required to leave Nazareth and go to Bethlehem to register there because Joseph belonged to the house and line of David. Both genealogies (Matt. 1, Luke 3), although differing in detail, are quite explicit on the point – Joseph was a descendant of David. There is an allusion to the same conviction in the fourth gospel – 'does not the Scripture say that Christ will come from David's family and from Bethlehem, the town where David lived?' (John 7:42). Jesus has many titles in the gospels – Rabbi, Lord, Master, Son of God, Son of Man, but this is the one and only occasion in St Mark when he is addressed publicly by the title 'Son of David'.

The Messianic secret

Perhaps this is the point at which to refer to an issue which was very prominent in the theological schools when I was a student and a teacher. It is called, in a kind of academic shorthand, 'the Messianic secret'. It arises out of a simple observation in Mark's gospel itself. At Mark 9:9 the disciples are strictly commanded not to tell anyone what happened on the Mount of Transfiguration until the Son of Man had risen from the dead. Jesus imposes the same command of silence upon the demons (e.g. Mark 1:34; 3:12). In Mark's view demons had supernatural knowledge. So the 'Messianic secret' is divulged to them but they are not allowed to witness to it in public.

The disciples, with the advantage of long companionship with Jesus, begin to penetrate to the same secret but are forbidden to speak of it in public. It has been deduced from this that the command to silence was a Marcan device for concealing the unwelcome truth that before the resurrection the thought that Jesus was, or might be, the Messiah had never occurred to anyone; it was wholly the product of early Christian theology.

But there may be a simpler solution to hand. The encounter with Bartimaeus illustrates it. The term 'Son of David' is a straight declaration of Jesus's natural descent from David. But by the time of the first century the term had acquired overtones which were not only misleading but dangerous. The 'Psalms of Solomon' current in Jesus's time made much of the coming Messiah who would be a son of David:

> Behold, O Lord, and raise up unto them their King, the son of David, at the time you have foreseen, O God, to rule over Israel your servant, and gird him with strength to shatter unrighteous rulers, and purge Jerusalem from the nations that trample her in destruction (Psalms of Solomon 17:21–2).

It was dreams like this that filled the imagination of first-century Judaism. The term, therefore, 'Son of David', would have been wholly unwelcome to Jesus because it created expectations widely removed from his own vision of his mission on earth, and indeed dangerous to it because of the likely reaction of the political authorities of the time. There were many so-called 'Messiahs' or 'Sons of David' who raised up an enthusiastic following, promised deliverance from the Romans, and suffered the inevitable penalty. Jesus would indeed suffer the penalty, but he could never preach a kingdom of the crude, militaristic sort which dominated the imagination of his people. It makes the manner of his entry into Jerusalem all the more pointed. He could not quench the enthusiasm of the Galilean pilgrims who had accompanied him to Bethany, but he would make it as clear as he possibly could that he was a man of peace, coming on a peaceful mission, riding on an ass and claiming no rights or privileges for himself. He was not a warrior king.

Bartimaeus

Bartimaeus would no doubt have been aware of his nation's expectations. The term 'Son of David' meant to him what it meant to most of his people – the triumph of a down-trodden people over their oppressors. But he was blind and helpless, wholly dependent on the charity of others. He had no political ambitions. Three times a year he would take up his pitch on the road out of Jericho to Jerusalem, hoping for a modest income. When he heard the noise, and became aware of the quite exceptional clamour which attended this particular pilgrim party he forgot the coins rattling in his box and reached for the stars. He had it on the authority of Scripture, which presumably he had never read, but would have heard in the synagogue, that when the Messiah came he would open the eyes of the blind:

> Then will the eyes of the blind be opened and the ears of the deaf unstopped. Then will the lame leap like a deer and the mute tongue shout for joy. Water will gush forth in the wilderness and streams in the desert. (Isa. 35:5–6)

The name of Jesus would not have been unfamiliar to him. He could not have sat year after year as pilgrims from Galilee passed by without picking up a rumour here, a bit of gossip there, about the miracles that were happening in that – to him – distant land. So he may indeed have used the vocabulary of his people, 'Son of David', but he was not looking for some national uprising which would throw off the yoke of Rome. He was blind and helpless and would remain so whoever reigned in Rome or ruled in Jerusalem. His joy knew no bounds when he was summoned into the presence of this man from Galilee, and he was astonished when in an instant the world opened before him in all its splendour and variety.

This is one of the few instances in the gospel when the name of the person is recorded – presumably because his name was known in the early Church as the member of one of the little Christian congregations in Jerusalem or Ephraim, in Bethany or Jericho. So with all the enthusiasm of his newfound sight, he left his box and his cloak behind him and followed Jesus 'in the way'. He did not need to be called: he followed. He did not need to be instructed or persuaded: he was eager to declare his allegiance to the one who could 'open the eyes of the blind and unstop the ears of the deaf, make the lame leap like a deer and the tongue of the dumb shout for joy'. In Mark's mind Bartimaeus was the ideal disciple, a model for the members of the Church for which he was writing.

13

THE CLEANSING OF THE TEMPLE

[Mark 11:15–19 and 27–33]

[15]On reaching Jerusalem, Jesus entered the temple area and began driving out those who were buying and selling there. He overturned the tables of the money changers and the benches of those selling doves, [16]and would not allow anyone to carry merchandise through the temple courts. [17]And as he taught them, he said, "Is it not written:

> " 'My house will be called
> a house of prayer for all nations'?

But you have made it 'a den of robbers'."
[18]The chief priests and the teachers of the law heard this and began looking for a way to kill him, for they feared him, because the whole crowd was amazed at his teaching.
[19]When evening came, they went out of the city. . .

[27]They arrived again in Jerusalem, and while Jesus was walking in the temple courts, the chief priests, the teachers of the law and the elders came to him. [28]"By what authority are you doing these things?" they asked. "And who gave you authority to do this?"
[29]Jesus replied, "I will ask you one question. Answer me, and I will tell you by what authority I am doing these things. [30]John's baptism —was it from heaven, or from men? Tell me!"
[31]They discussed it among themselves and said, "If we say, 'From heaven,' he will ask, 'Then why didn't you believe him?' [32]But if we say, 'From men'. . . ." (They feared the people, for everyone held that John really was a prophet.)
[33]So they answered Jesus, "We don't know."
Jesus said, "Neither will I tell you by what authority I am doing these things."

It is less than twenty miles from Jericho to Jerusalem, but any traveller, ancient or modern, would be struck by the sharp contrasts between them. Jericho is in the Jordan valley, at this point some three thousand feet below sea-level, in the grip of a hot, enervating climate which nevertheless provides a rich soil and plentiful water. It abounds with fruit-trees and crops of every kind. It was, as George Adam Smith said, 'the Larder' for the whole area around it. The traveller will ascend by more than three thousand feet by the time he reaches the Mount of Olives overlooking Jerusalem. In the winter snow can fall in Jerusalem and the weather can be uncomfortably cold and wet. Even at the height of the summer the heat is never overpowering and is tempered by a brisk wind.

Jerusalem

The change of climate may come as a benediction to the traveller, but it has other consequences for those who actually inhabit the city. The soil is poor, the water-supply for long periods of its history was inadequate, and it was always at risk from famine, especially if the number of its inhabitants was swollen by fear of war. Unlike Galilee, from which Jesus came, it did not stand on any international trade route, and such industries as it had were of the small backroom kind, not very different from what can still be seen in the bazaars of the ancient city.

But it had some assets which Jericho lacked. Once the water-supply had been improved by Hezekiah and subsequent rulers of Judah, the hill on which the city was built was capable of being made into a formidable military stronghold, and it had from time immemorial been a centre of worship. It appears in the earliest records of Israel as 'Salem' from which Melchizedek, king and priest, brought bread and wine for Abraham and blessed him in the name of God most high, creator of both heaven and earth (Gen. 14:18–19). Archaeological finds on the hill of Ophel suggest that as early as 2,500 BC it was a walled city.

It achieved prominence in the history of Israel from the time that it was captured by David and became not only the capital of his kingdom but a centre of worship. It served as a permanent home for the Ark of God containing the two

tablets of stone (2 Sam. 6:6–10); round it in Solomon's time
there developed a large and impressive Temple, sedulously
served by the priests employed in the sacrificial system.

It achieved a certain symbolic importance in the political
and international rivalries of the ancient world, but suffered
in consequence from constant threats of invasion and the
occasional siege. It was occupied by Babylonian forces in 598
BC and was levelled to the ground in 587 BC. Rebuilt within a
century, it became the centre of administration for the return-
ing exiles, and reached its zenith in the time of Herod the
Great who, out of regard for the religious susceptibilities
of his Jewish subjects, greatly enlarged and beautified the
Temple, and out of regard for his political masters in
Rome, adorned the city with a theatre, a gymnasium and a
hippodrome.

The Temple

The city which Jesus entered in triumphal procession on Palm
Sunday was, however, no longer just a political or adminis-
trative centre for Israel. It was the centre of a worldwide
religion, created by the dispersal of the Jews throughout the
cities of the Mediterranean and Asia Minor. It was the hub of
a complex religious system which drew pilgrims from all over
the world three times a year in their tens of thousands. It is
estimated that the city had a mere 25,000 inhabitants, but that
it was swollen to an unimaginable degree by the influx of
pilgrims, especially for the Passover, numbering about
125,000. This had huge consequences for the city. With no
industries worth speaking of, with limited agricultural resources, and with no world trade to sustain it, it became more
and more dependent on the pilgrim traffic.

It was one of the first cities in the world to develop tourism
on a large scale – with all the consequent disadvantages. It
acquired a reputation for overcharging for accommodation,
for putting the prices up during the pilgrim season and for
exacting quite extortionate rates of interest on the exchange
of money required for the payment of the Temple dues. The

Temple itself became a source of profit to those, the high priest and others, who controlled it.

The sight which greeted Jesus and his followers when they arrived in Jerusalem was to them a singularly unedifying one, contrasting painfully with the reputation the city enjoyed as the holy dwelling-place of God. It exhibited all the evidences of greed and corruption. It had become a 'den of robbers' to the pilgrims who made their way from the farthest points of the known world. They would have been in danger throughout their journey from robbers and highwaymen. If they were lucky enough to escape unscathed on their journey they were certain to be robbed when they got to their journey's end. The poor man, who had sacrificed everything to make the pilgrimage, lost what little was left when he got there. Jesus's action, therefore, may not have been planned long before. It may have been a spontaneous prophetic action, expressing the wrath of God against the ruthless exploitation of the poor, practised by those who were nominally his servants and representatives. Amos had had much the same to say at the northern shrine at Bethel in his day:

> Come to Bethel, and transgress; to Gilgal, and multiply transgression; bring your sacrifices every morning, your tithes every three days; offer a sacrifice of thanksgiving of that which is leavened, and proclaim freewill offerings, publish them. (Amos 4:4–5 RSV)

The reaction to him was much the same as it was to be to Jesus:

> Then Amaziah the priest of Bethel sent a message to Jeroboam King of Israel: 'Amos is raising a conspiracy against you in the very heart of Israel. The land cannot bear all his words. For this is what Amos is saying:
> "Jeroboam will die by the sword, and Israel will surely go into exile, away from their native land."' Then Amaziah said to Amos, 'Get out, you seer! Go back to the land of Judah. Earn your bread there and do your prophesying there. Don't prophesy any more at Bethel, because this is the king's sanctuary and the temple of the kingdom.' (Amos 7:10–13)

But Jesus's action was more than a protest, in the true prophetic line, against formality of religion and corruption of worship. It was a furious indictment of the whole Jerusalem establishment, made all the more threatening by its conjunction with his triumphal entry into Jerusalem two days earlier. After all, he had not entered Jerusalem as Amos had entered Bethel with rough clothing and a stick in his hand, and alone. He had entered riding on an ass with a great retinue of followers crying 'Hosannah to the Son of David'. It was a Messianic demonstration which had been launched from Bethany and it must have seemed to the powers-that-be a dangerous Messianic gesture which was enacted in the Temple precincts. The establishment could hardly ignore it without exposing themselves to the charge that they were indeed corrupt stewards of God's gifts, unworthy representatives of his grace. Furthermore, it had placed them in an invidious position in relation to the Roman procurator who was notoriously sensitive to dangers of riot and disturbance during the great festivals of the Jewish year.

The rulers of Israel

The cleansing of the Temple was a challenge the rulers of Israel could not ignore. So now is the moment to consider who these rulers of Israel were and how they had achieved their pre-eminence in the life of Israel, not only in Judea, Peraea or Galilee but in the Jewish communities scattered all over the world.

It was customary in Israel to trace every distinctive institution in the nation back to Moses. Moses was the archetypal ruler of the people, bringing them out of Israel with a strong hand and seeing them safely through the wilderness. He was the giver of the Law and the infallible interpreter of it. He laid the foundations of the sacrificial system and inaugurated the priesthood. He even created a primitive Sanhedrin (Exod. 18:25). He was the prophet without rival (Deut. 34:10).

The one distinctive institution in Israel which Moses did not create was the monarchy, and indeed he specifically warned them against it (Deut. 17:14–20). The credit for this, according to the author of 1 Samuel, goes to Samuel, but the author himself is clearly ambivalent about it. There are two accounts of the founding of the monarchy which he makes no attempt to harmonise. The one account beginning in chapter 8 describes how, when Samuel grew old and his sons did not walk in his ways, the elders of Israel sent a deputation to Samuel urging him to find them a king who would take over when he died. '. . . this displeased Samuel;' so the narrative runs, 'so he prayed to the Lord. And the Lord told him: "Listen to all that the people are saying to you; it is not you they have rejected, but they have rejected me as their king"' (1 Sam. 8:6–7). The other account is much more picturesque; it tells how a young man, Saul, was sent out looking for his father's asses, failed to find them and fell in 'by accident' with Samuel, who, having been forewarned of God, anointed him the first king of Israel (1 Sam. 9). One account thus suggests that the monarchy was the result of an illegitimate demand by the elders of Israel, the other that it was the direct will of God communicated to his prophet.

This ambivalence persisted throughout Israel's history. The kings, with some notable exceptions, proved to be rapacious or ineffective or both. They patently did not honour or enforce the Law which was supposed to be the basis of their government, and they were sometimes fatally compromised by their relationship with other nations and with other religions.

The royal line of David expired at the total collapse of Jerusalem in 586 BC. The monarchy was revived by the Hasmonaeans, descendants of the Maccabees, and Jesus himself was born when Herod, part-Edomite, part-Jew, was on the throne of Israel. But neither the Hasmonaeans nor Herod could claim to be of the House of David, and so in troubled times there rose to the surface of Jewish life a fond hope that one day in God's own time there would arise from the House of David the king of their dreams, who would throw off the foreign yoke and dispense justice once again from Zion. It was this hope that was reflected in the phrase

'Son of David' by which Jesus was acclaimed on his entry into Jerusalem.

Thus it was that there arose in Israel, centuries before Christ, a certain tension between what we may call the 'Messianic dream' and the regime which actually ruled Israel from Jerusalem. It is a variation of the frequent motif in Hebrew history of the conflict between the prophet and the institution. It was this age-old conflict which surfaced dramatically in the cleansing of the Temple. Jesus, a prophet from Galilee and a crypto-Messiah, now confronted the principalities and powers of the world in the city of David.

Jewry, at home and abroad, was for all practical purposes ruled by what was called the Sanhedrin, which means in the Hebrew language 'Court'. It may surprise the reader that we do not know precisely how the Sanhedrin was composed, or where the balance of power lay in it. We do know that it numbered 70, 71 or 72 in all, and that it was the High Priest who presided over it when it was in full session. The office of High Priest was hereditary, and for life. It was of the greatest possible importance in the religion of Israel, because only the duly-appointed High Priest could perform the essential office on the Day of Atonement, of entering the holy of holies to make atonement for himself and for the people. But by virtue of his office he also came to be regarded as spokesman for the nation and it was he who had to negotiate with the various conquerors (Greek, Seleucid, Roman) to whom Israel was from time to time subject. Thus the office acquired a certain political significance which became an important element in the uneasy relationship between the Roman empire and worldwide Judaism.

In the century before the fall of Jerusalem in AD 70 there were no less than twenty-eight High Priests. They were installed and removed at will by their overlords and were by the time of Jesus entirely dependent on the goodwill and support of the procurator. So while still regarded as the linchpin of the religion of Israel, their image was seriously tarnished by the compromises and the subterfuges, not to say the bribes, by which they gained or retained office. Caiaphas, the present High Priest, was luckier than most; he retained his office for eighteen years, from AD 18–37. His father-in-law, Annas, had been High Priest from AD 6–15, and was now one among several of what are called 'the chief priests', who constituted a specific grouping within the Sanhedrin as a whole.

Then there were the 'Elders', men of wealth and substance from the ancient families of Jerusalem, who constituted a powerful lay element on the Sanhedrin.

The third main group in the council were the Scribes, otherwise called 'lawyers' or 'doctors of the law'. They had risen to a position of leadership in Israel after the exile when Ezra, the scribe from Babylon, acted as a kind of second Moses, seeking to re-establish the life of Israel on the basis of meticulous obedience to the Law. These men had received a rigorous training in the Law, were formally ordained, and were treated with great reverence by the people, being called 'Rabbi', 'Master' or 'Lord'. They occupied an important position not only in the religious but in the social life of Israel.

The Sanhedrin

In the first century AD the Sanhedrin still enjoyed great prestige as the sole, national governing body, but it is not difficult to imagine the compromises that were required to sustain its cohesion. The High Priest himself was often little more than a creature of the imperial government, concerned above all to safeguard his position. The chief priests no doubt often looked down on the latest occupant of the high priestly office with disdain. The elders or the 'lay nobility' (as they are sometimes called) were perhaps among those who eagerly welcomed the theatre and the gymnasium, and the sports centres which were the mark of a civilised Roman society, while others of them, in the name of ancient tradition, bitterly resisted them.

The Scribes, for their part, were often divided among themselves on questions of doctrine, some embracing the Sadducean position, for example that there was no resurrection – some adhering to the Pharisaic belief in the resurrection and the last day. But all of them would have placed high among their priorities the integrity and unity of the people of God. Caiaphas was probably expressing the opinion of most of them when he said: 'If we let him [Christ] go on like this, everyone will believe in him, and then the Romans will come and take away both our place and our nation' (John 11:48).

So Jesus's action in the Temple precincts presented in one way or another a serious challenge to the Sanhedrin and to every group within it. They had everything to lose. Small wonder that they began looking for a way to silence him. The Sanhedrin distinctly did not welcome the Messiah; they had grown used to the thought that the Messiah would come at the end of time, and did not relish having a son of David to rule over them here and now.

The great institutional churches of our own day, secure in their learning, wealth and social position, never find it easy to welcome a 'Messiah'. They may say, with genuine conviction, that 'he will come again with glory to judge both the quick and the dead' but, preferably, not yet.

The cleansing of the Temple

John placed the cleansing of the Temple at the beginning of Jesus's ministry (John 2:12–25). For John, therefore, the event which provoked the fierce reaction from the Jewish leaders was not the cleansing of the Temple, but the raising of Lazarus. We have to allow for the fact that, with Mark's foreshortened view of the ministry, he records only one visit to Jerusalem: it follows, therefore, that the cleansing must of necessity have taken place then.

But even allowing for that 'necessity' I incline to the view that Mark's version of events is correct. It was not the miracle of the raising of Lazarus but the explicit threat to their authority with the cleansing of the Temple which convinced the Sanhedrin that it was time for action. At this point, therefore, we have to ask our usual question – what did Mark himself intend to convey to the Church of his own time and in his own place?

Given the fact that he was writing in the late sixties of the first century he, and his readers in Rome, would have been only too well aware of the revolt against the empire which was gathering momentum in Israel and was to culminate in the fall of Jerusalem in AD 70. It was important therefore that both the Church and the imperial authorities should recognise that the rulers of the Jewish people had already shown themselves hostile to Jesus and had themselves initiated the legal proceedings against him which led to his death. It was important that the Christians should not be seen to be implicated in the Jewish revolt.

It is beyond dispute that the rulers of the Jews were hostile to Jesus and subsequently to the Church, but the political situation certainly caused Mark to emphasise it. That is why throughout the gospel various delegations comprising chief priests, elders, scribes, teachers of the Law, lawyers, are frequently shown in confrontation with Jesus. The cleansing of the Temple is just the most dramatic confrontation among many others.

But Mark would have had in mind also the hostility which Paul and other missionaries of the gospel had experienced in Asia Minor and Greece among the Jewish communities in which they first ministered. Mark's gospel would therefore provide an important illustration of the fact that any opposition they received from the local 'rulers of the Jews' was a reflection of the hostility which Jesus himself had experienced. This was particularly important in a Christian community comprising both Gentiles and converted Jews. But perhaps the most important point which Mark has to make in this particular passage is expressed in the argument which arose after the cleansing of the Temple regarding Jesus's authority.

The authority of Jesus

The authority of Jesus would have been a matter of great concern to any congregation composed of converted Jews and Gentiles. After all, what authority did he have to overturn the tables of the money-changers and the benches of those selling doves? By what right did he call the Temple 'a den of robbers'? Who was this little-known rabbi from Galilee who dared to confront the chief priest, the lay nobility and the learned scribes of worldwide Jewry? Long before intellectual questions arose in the Church regarding the exact nature of Christ and his relationship with the Father, those early Christians were bound to ask themselves – how do we come to attribute all authority in heaven and earth to this humble artisan from Nazareth? (Matt. 28:18). Mark had begun the gospel with a quotation from the prophet Malachi. Here is the passage from which he quotes:

'See, I will send my messenger, who will prepare the way before me. Then suddenly the Lord you are seeking will come to his temple; the messenger of the covenant, whom you desire, will come,' says the Lord Almighty. But who can endure the day of his coming? Who can stand when he appears? For he will be like a refiner's fire or a launderer's soap. He will sit as a refiner and purifier of silver; he will purify the Levites and refine them like gold and silver. Then the Lord will have men who will bring offerings in righteousness, and the offerings of Judah and Jerusalem will be acceptable to the Lord, as in days gone by, as in former years. (Mal. 3:1–4)

So, Mark is saying, 'the messenger' had already come in the person of John the Baptist preparing the way of the Lord, but now the Lord himself had come to the Temple to cleanse it and to re-establish it in truth and purity. When the rulers of Israel plotted against him they were not plotting against a prophet; they were resisting the Messiah himself and in so doing were resisting God. Jesus's answer to the question they were asking him was not just a clever debating point but an attempt to expose them once more to the truth implied by the coming of John the Baptist, in tradition, the 'Elijah' who would herald the coming of the King and the Kingdom. If they had believed in him as a real messenger of God then they would have believed in the one to whom he bore witness, and they would have opened the gates of Jerusalem itself to let in the King of glory.

The Lord indeed had suddenly come to his Temple and

they were not ready for him. The rulers of the nations and the rulers of the Church come under the same condemnation, when they think or say 'we don't want this man to be our king' (Luke 19 v. 14). The cleansing of the Temple was what they had frequently demanded – a sign from heaven. But they did not recognise it.

14

THE WOMAN AT BETHANY

[Mark 14:1–11]

14 Now the Passover and the Feast of Unleavened Bread were only two days away, and the chief priests and the teachers of the law were looking for some sly way to arrest Jesus and kill him. [2]"But not during the Feast," they said, "or the people may riot."

[3]While he was in Bethany, reclining at the table in the home of a man known as Simon the Leper, a woman came with an alabaster jar of very expensive perfume, made of pure nard. She broke the jar and poured the perfume on his head.

[4]Some of those present were saying indignantly to one another, "Why this waste of perfume? [5]It could have been sold for more than a year's wages and the money given to the poor." And they rebuked her harshly.

[6]"Leave her alone," said Jesus. "Why are you bothering her? She has done a beautiful thing to me. [7]The poor you will always have with you, and you can help them any time you want. But you will not always have me. [8]She did what she could. She poured perfume on my body beforehand to prepare for my burial. [9]I tell you the truth, wherever the gospel is preached throughout the world, what she has done will also be told, in memory of her."

[10]Then Judas Iscariot, one of the Twelve, went to the chief priests to betray Jesus to them. [11]They were delighted to hear this and promised to give him money. So he watched for an opportunity to hand him over.

The dispute about the authority of Jesus referred to in the last chapter heralds a series of disputes with which by now Jesus was painfully familiar. His ministry opened with a series of disputes with the local Jewish authorities in Galilee, recorded in Mark, chapters 1 and 2, and often referred to as 'the conflict stories'. Then it had been conflict about the laws of purification (1:40–45), about the right to forgive sins (2:1–12), about rules of table fellowship (2:15–17), about the custom of fasting (2:18–22), and about the laws of Sabbath observance (2:22–3:6). At the end of the conflict stories Mark records that 'Jesus withdrew' (3:7). But now there can be no withdrawal. He is in Jerusalem in obedience to his Father's will, and now confronts not the local Jewish authorities in Galilee but the national and religious Jewish authorities in the holy city itself.

Public Controversy

The controversy about his authority to 'cleanse the Temple' plunges him into another series of 'conflict stories'. He tells them a parable about a man who planted a vineyard and let it out to tenants; but when he sent his servants to collect the fruit of the vineyard they were roughly treated; when, as a last resort he sent his son, they killed him. Representatives of the Sanhedrin who heard the parable rightly perceived that he had spoken the parable against them as the tenants of the Lord's vineyard, and they looked for a way to arrest him (Mark 12:12).

This is followed by an embassy of Pharisees and Herodians who try to provoke him to the kind of utterance which would incriminate him in the eyes of the Roman governor. They only succeeded in provoking a comment which has echoed down the centuries and is as relevant now as it was then – 'give to Caesar what is Caesar's and to God what is God's' (12:17). Then the Sadducees took their turn: they confronted him with the vexed question of life beyond the grave (about which they were in dispute with the Pharisees). At a stroke their complicated theology yields to one of the great utterances of Jesus – 'God is not the God of the dead, but of the living' (12:27).

The next would-be debater was a teacher of the Law asking which of the commandments was the most important. On the whole this group of conflict stories exhibits Jesus in what must have been a familiar role – a skilled debater, learned in the Law, eager to recover for God's people the true meaning of the Law so long buried beneath the disputes of the official teachers of the Law. The section comes to an end with a solemn warning – 'Watch out for the teachers of the law. They like to walk around in flowing robes and be greeted in the market-places, and have the most important seats in the synagogues and the places of honour at banquets. They devour widows' houses and for a show make lengthy prayers. Such men will be punished most severely' (12:38–40).

The Judgment on Jerusalem

I never read that passage myself without a certain discomfort. I have known what it is to walk around in flowing robes and be greeted in the market-places, to have the most important seats in the church, the place of honour at banquets. If to the best of my knowledge I have not devoured widows' houses, I am painfully aware of the spiritual dangers to which religious prestige exposes the 'teacher of the law'.

All these disputes are located by Mark in the court of the Temple which was habitually used for teaching and debate. The debates in which Jesus had been engaged were not in his view academic matters, of interest only to theologians; in Jesus's mind they were matters of life and death, for example, the sanctity of God's house, the proper care of God's people, the reality of life beyond death. But it was evident to him now that the guardians of the nation's life were more concerned with power and prestige, with personal advantage and wealth. When, therefore, the disciples, on their way out, drew his attention to the splendid buildings of the Temple, Jesus was not impressed. '"Do you see all these great buildings?" replied Jesus. "Not one stone here will be left on another, every one will be thrown down"' (Mark 13:2).

The holy city had resisted and would reject the Messiah, and would pay the ultimate cost of that rejection. It was a grim warning and within forty years it was fulfilled. At the end of the Jewish revolt in AD 70 the walls had been torn down and the Temple desecrated. No more flowing robes for the teachers of the Law to walk about in, no markets in which to be greeted, no synagogues in which to occupy important seats, no banquets in which to take the place of honour. The official opponents of Jesus may have won a few battles but they certainly lost the war: within a hundred years the city had been rebuilt as a Roman military camp and was wholly given over to the worship of Jupiter.

How the gospels vary

This introduction is necessary for the understanding of the incident with which we are now concerned – the anointing of Jesus in Bethany. It is an act of private devotion in deliberate contrast with the bitter public controversies which preceded it.

As far as possible in this book I have tried to concentrate attention on Mark's understanding of Jesus, and have tried to exclude from my own mind material which is lodged in it from the other gospels. But now if we are to distinguish Mark's understanding of this incident in Bethany we need to be aware of parallel narratives in the other gospels, by way of comparison and contrast.

I begin with Matthew's gospel as being the closest to Mark in outline (Matt. 26:6–13). Both gospels agree that the encounter took place in Bethany in the house of Simon the Leper. Mark says that it was 'some of those who were present' who objected to the waste of the perfume. Matthew is more explicit and says that it was the disciples who were indignant about it. Mark is explicit about the value of the perfume. Matthew is content to say that it could have been sold for much. Mark says that the woman broke the jar – a detail omitted by Matthew. You will see that the variations between these two gospels are few and of little account: Matthew on the whole follows his source faithfully.

I turn next to John (12:1–8). Here there are substantial, indeed, significant differences. For one thing Mark's unstated chronology suggests that the anointing took place on the Wednesday, whereas John says that it was six days before the Passover which on John's reckoning would mean the previous Saturday. The dinner was given in Bethany, but Simon the Leper is not mentioned. All that is said is that Martha served while Lazarus was among those reclining at the table.

In Mark and Matthew the woman who anointed Jesus is not named, but in John it is Mary, the sister of Martha and Lazarus. Mark says that it was some of the people present who objected to the waste, Matthew says that it was the disciples. John is even more explicit: it was Judas Iscariot who objected. The two accounts are not wholly incompatible with each other, apart from the question of date, but there are certainly substantial differences in detail, and there is no obvious way of reconciling them.

More serious problems arise however, out of Luke's account of an anointing in Luke 7:36–50. This anointing occupies a quite different place in the narrative. It comes in the earliest stages of Jesus's ministry, as part of the Galilean section. The dinner takes place at the house of Simon the Pharisee. The woman concerned is a prostitute and 'she stood behind him at his feet weeping, she began to wet his feet with her tears. Then she wiped them with her hair, kissed them and poured perfume on them' (Luke 7:38). The action gave rise to a discourse on a quite different theme, culminating in the memorable words – 'I tell you her many sins have been forgiven – for she loved much. But he who has been forgiven little loves little' (Luke 7:47).

Why the gospels vary

As you can imagine these variations in the narrative, major and minor, have produced among the older commentators on the Bible many ingenious suggestions. Origen, for once in a way defeated by the problem, can only offer the possibility that there were three different anointings. Augustine suggested that the same woman anointed Jesus twice, once early on in Galilee and a second time in Bethany.

In some ways the proposed solutions are more of a problem than the problem itself. The evangelists were not composing their respective gospels on the basis of assured chronological or geographical information. They had to do their best with a large collection, oral and written, of reminiscences current in the apostolic age. There was no national library to which they could refer; they had no research assistants. It is unlikely that any of them were actually involved in the events which they record. Rather, therefore, than attempting to reconcile the irreconcilable, it would be wiser to take seriously the fact that the evangelists were writing at intervals of as much as thirty or forty years from each other; that they belonged to congregations widely separated from each other; that they drew on different sources of information; and that they had quite different objectives in mind.

This is illustrated in this present instance by the simple fact that Luke deliberately omits the story of the anointing in Bethany because he is aware of having already recorded the story of an anointing in Galilee. There may have been two such anointings, but Luke obviously does not believe so. We are in no position to judge why he should choose the one story and omit the other, but it is interesting to observe elsewhere in Luke a certain ambivalence about events at Bethany.

In what we call Holy Week Mark says that Jesus went out of the city each night back to Bethany; Luke says no more than that he returned to the Mount of Olives. Mark is clearly aware of the fact, which John confirms, that Bethany provided Jesus with the only home he had in the Jerusalem area and that he presumably stayed there on his visits to the city. Luke, like John, is aware of Jesus's friendship with Martha and Mary, but the only meeting he records is in the earlier part of the ministry in 'a village' which is unnamed (Luke 10:38–42). Mark does not mention Martha and Mary at all.

Such apparent disparities certainly make for confusion, but for illumination also: for a moment we are permitted to go behind the scenes, to receive an insight into the minds of the evangelists, their sources of information and their distinctive views of the man whom they so lovingly describe. They refract the light; they speak out of their own time and are subject to their own limitations; they emphasise now one aspect of the truth, then another aspect. Not presuming to possess the totality of truth, they are content with their, admittedly partial, sometimes even partisan, view of it. What impresses me about the gospels is not their unanimity in matters of detail, but their comprehensive and indeed 'synoptic' presentation of the one who defeats all attempts to encompass him, who has eluded the grasp of men infinitely greater than the evangelists, and yet who comes to life, vividly and unforgettably, in the pages of the New Testament.

An act of loving devotion

Now we are in a better position to ask the question: What did Mark, the earliest of the evangelists, understand by this event, and what does he imply by the way in which he presents it? We have seen that it is placed here probably deliberately as a contrast with the scenes depicted in the previous two chapters. In the courts of the Temple, the holy city of Jerusalem, the 'joy of the whole earth', Jesus is confronted with the wilful misunderstanding and the bitter hostility of those who were supposed to be the guardians of the nation's life. There, he was at the mercy of small-minded men with a large opinion of their own importance, but with little knowledge, so it seemed, of the grand purposes for which Israel had been chosen by God. They were content to enjoy the luxury of public prestige, but they were devoid of vision and intolerant in spirit. They were, as Jesus said, 'blind leaders of the blind'.

By contrast, within a few hours, he finds himself no longer in the hallowed courts of the Temple, but in the house of Simon the Leper. The people he would be consorting with there would have been despised by the proud rulers of Jerusalem, as 'people without the Law'. But in the company of those who ate that day in Simon's house there was a woman capable of acts of generosity and devotion which were quite beyond the range of those who sat in Moses' seat. She is given no name, but her unexpected memorial is that 'wherever the gospel is preached throughout the world what she has done will also be told in memory of her' (Mark 14:9).

Was she one of the women who had accompanied Jesus on his travels and provided the necessary financial resources (Matt. 27:56); was she Mary of Magdala from whom seven devils had been cast out (Mark 16:9); or do we accept the only positive identification we have and say with John that it was Mary, sister of Martha and Lazarus? We shall never know, but we do know that the action which was regarded by some of the guests as a gross extravagance was received by Jesus for what it was – a lavish gift out of a generous heart, an expression of love and devotion which was signally absent from his reception elsewhere in the holy city. Judas was to be remembered for his treachery, Caiaphas for his cynical abuse of power, Pilate for a flagrant breach of justice: this unnamed woman was to be remembered throughout the world wherever the gospel was preached for her simple, spontaneous, uncalculating act of love.

A coronation

But for Mark it was more than that. It needs to be observed that Mark, followed by Matthew, makes it clear that the woman anointed Jesus's head. John, in the parallel narrative, and Luke in his own earlier version of the story, say no more than that she anointed Jesus's feet. This might seem to the reader to be a small point, but to Mark it was all-important. The anointing was not just an act of common courtesy which might be offered to any distinguished guest. It was a coronation. The anointing of the head was part of the ritual of the coronation service for the kings of Israel (1 Sam. 10:1; 16:13).

The term Messiah means simply 'the anointed one', and, as we have seen already, the general expectation in the centuries before the Christian era was that the Messiah would be of the house of David and would rule over his people with justice and clemency. So in Mark's mind the anointing is just another 'sign of the Messiah', not a sign from heaven, but a secret sign, not a grand, liturgical occasion in the Temple of the most high God, but in the living-room in the house of Simon the Leper.

The author of the gospel might have said at this point, as he had said before (Mark 13:14), 'let the reader understand'. From the beginning, Mark's understanding of Jesus had not been of the triumphant Messiah who would reign in glory over his people on earth, but rather of the suffering and crucified Messiah who would reign over the whole created order from heaven. So it is particularly significant to Mark that it is Jesus himself who makes the connection between his 'coronation' and his death – 'she did what she could, she poured perfume on my body beforehand to prepare for my burial' (14:8).

There is a curious intensity about this passage which I have not felt so markedly in any of the previous 'encounters'; it is due not to the subtle or dramatic use of language, or to literary skill; it is simply integral to the event. There is a sense in which it expresses Mark's mind on the whole meaning of the gospel, and it is no accident that this is one of the few occasions on which the word 'gospel' is used by Mark, since he used it in the words of his title: 'The beginning of the gospel about Jesus Christ, the Son of God' (Mark 1:1). It is the Messiah, already anointed, who receives the crown of thorns, and ascends the throne at Calvary. The 'Messianic secret', so long hidden from the disciples, still hidden from the rulers of Israel, is disclosed by the action of an unknown woman in the house of Simon the Leper.

15

JUDAS

[Mark 14:32–52]

³²They went to a place called Gethsemane, and Jesus said to his disciples, "Sit here while I pray." ³³He took Peter, James and John along with him, and he began to be deeply distressed and troubled. ³⁴"My soul is overwhelmed with sorrow to the point of death," he said to them. "Stay here and keep watch."

³⁵Going a little farther, he fell to the ground and prayed that if possible the hour might pass from him. ³⁶"*Abba*, Father," he said, "everything is possible for you. Take this cup from me. Yet not what I will, but what you will."

³⁷Then he returned to his disciples and found them sleeping. "Simon," he said to Peter, "are you asleep? Could you not keep watch for one hour? ³⁸Watch and pray so that you will not fall into temptation. The spirit is willing, but the body is weak."

³⁹Once more he went away and prayed the same thing. ⁴⁰When he came back, he again found them sleeping, because their eyes were heavy. They did not know what to say to him.

⁴¹Returning the third time, he said to them, "Are you still sleeping and resting? Enough! The hour has come. Look, the Son of Man is betrayed into the hands of sinners. ⁴²Rise! Let us go! Here comes my betrayer!"

⁴³Just as he was speaking, Judas, one of the Twelve, appeared. With him was a crowd armed with swords and clubs, sent from the chief priests, the teachers of the law, and the elders.

⁴⁴Now the betrayer had arranged a signal with them: "The one I kiss is the man; arrest him and lead him away under guard." ⁴⁵Going at once to Jesus, Judas said, "Rabbi!" and kissed him. ⁴⁶The men seized Jesus and arrested him. ⁴⁷Then one of those standing near drew his sword and struck the servant of the high priest, cutting off his ear.

⁴⁸"Am I leading a rebellion," said Jesus, "that you have come out with swords and clubs to capture me? ⁴⁹Every day I was with you, teaching in the temple courts, and you did not arrest me. But the Scriptures must be fulfilled." ⁵⁰Then everyone deserted him and fled.

⁵¹A young man, wearing nothing but a linen garment, was following Jesus. When they seized him, ⁵²he fled naked, leaving his garment behind.

There could be two questions which an interested enquirer might well ask of the Church in the first century. The first would be: If Jesus truly was the Messiah, why was it that the leaders of his own people rejected him? This is a serious enough question, but there is an even more serious one. It is not difficult to see why the leaders of his people rejected him. They were conscious of their responsibilities for the Jewish race all over the world, they were understandably nervous of the reaction of the Roman authorities, not only in Jerusalem but throughout the empire, to any movement which appeared, however faintly, to be revolutionary. No doubt the Jewish leaders were animated also by less respectable considerations, for example, concern for their own authority, pride of learning, and nervousness, characteristic of the Church of all ages, in the face of popular enthusiasm. Thus their actions, while reprehensible, were intelligible.

But what of Judas? He was not involved in national or ecclesiastical politics. He had no authority which could be threatened, and he would hardly have joined the apostolic band if he had not had a certain enthusiasm for 'the kingdom'. Yet here was a man who answered the call of a teacher in whom he truly believed, and made the kind of sacrifice which all the apostles made, but who, with the full knowledge of what he was doing, and without any outside pressure, found it in his heart to betray Jesus. Of the two questions the would-be enquirer might ask, this would be far the more difficult one to answer satisfactorily. Difficult? The plain fact is that it has never been satisfactorily answered.

Judas in the early Church

It is interesting to observe that the problem becomes more rather than less difficult with the passage of time. Mark refers to Judas in his list of the apostles (Mark 3:19), but not again until after the anointing in Bethany, when he went to the chief priests to betray Jesus to them. Then follows the actual betrayal, but no account of his death. His name is mentioned in the first gospel only five times. Luke is almost equally reticent – six times; Matthew – eight times. But in St John's gospel, normally regarded as the last of the gospels, there are thirteen actual references and several allusions. In fact, it is John who is the only one to attempt any explanation of Judas's actions. His explanation arises not primarily out of historical considerations but theological ones, the chief one being that if Jesus really knew what was in the hearts of men why did he choose Judas in the first place, and why did he not, in the later stages of his ministry, anticipate the problem by excluding Judas from the fellowship of the Twelve?

John offers no explanation as such, but he does insist that Jesus had long perceived that there was indeed something in Judas which could ultimately lead to the betrayal:

> For Jesus had known from the beginning which of them did not believe and who would betray him. (John 6:64)
>
> 'Have I not chosen you, the Twelve? Yet one of you is a devil!' (He meant Judas, the son of Simon Iscariot, who, though one of the Twelve, was later to betray him). (John 6:70–1)
>
> 'And you are clean, though not every one of you.' For he knew who was going to betray him, and that was why he said not every one was clean. (John 13:10–11)

John, in common with Mark, does not mention the death of Judas. It was sufficient for his purpose to say that during supper, as soon as Judas had taken the bread, he went out. 'And it was night' (John 13:30). The Prince of Darkness had taken the son of darkness to his own.

Matthew and Luke do not offer any explanation of the betrayal. They are content to record his death as a sign of judgment upon him. Matthew records that Judas, seized with remorse, returned the thirty silver coins to the chief priests and the elders and went out and hanged himself (Matt. 27:5). Luke does not record his death in the gospel, but in the Acts of the Apostles, where an alternative story of his death is added to the story of the choice of Matthias to replace the traitor.

> With the reward he got for his wickedness, Judas bought a field; there he fell headlong, his body burst open and all his intestines spilled out. Everyone in Jerusalem heard about this, so they called that field in their language Akeldama, that is, Field of Blood. (Acts 1:18–19)

In the course of time the horror at Judas's action produced some grotesque accounts of his fate. One such comes from Papias (60–130):

> Judas walked about in this world a terrible example of impiety, his flesh swollen to such an extent that where a wagon can pass with ease he was not able to pass, no not even the mass of his head merely. They say that his eyelids swelled to such an extent that he could not see the light at all, while as for his eyes they were not visible even by a physician looking through an instrument, so far had they sunk from the surface.

In comparison, the evangelists treated the event in a restrained way, and none more restrained than the first evangelist, Mark.

The Last Supper

His attitude to the betrayal has to be seen in the context of the chronology he adopts for the whole week. On the first day (our Sunday) Jesus entered Jerusalem in triumph. On the second day (our Monday) he cleansed the Temple. On the third (our Tuesday) he engaged in disputes with the teachers of the Law. On the fourth day (our Wednesday) he is anointed in the home of Simon the Leper and Judas betrays him to the chief priests. On the fifth day (our Thursday) the disciples prepare for the last supper; Jesus joins them in an unidentified house in Jerusalem and Judas is present. On the Friday Jesus is crucified and is buried (before the onset of the Sabbath) and on the Sunday morning he rises from the dead.

There is little doubt that this corresponds to a genuine sequence of events which the other evangelists take more or less for granted. But you will observe that I have used the term 'last supper' in preference to 'Passover meal' for the Thursday evening. This is because we cannot be certain on which day of the week that year the Passover was celebrated. It is a matter of dispute, therefore, whether the supper was a Passover meal or whether it was just the 'last supper' with his disciples on earth.

This scarcely matters for our immediate purpose, but the Church has been divided on this issue from the beginning, chiefly regarding the nature of the Eucharist – whether it is or is not a Passover meal. The issue is made all the more complicated because the Jewish day, unlike the Roman day, begins at dusk. Thus Thursday is Thursday, but Friday begins in the evening. This has been a fruitful source of confusion, and not least, I must admit, to the author of this book.

What, however, is beyond dispute is that the death of Jesus took place on Friday and was associated with the Passover, whether it coincided with the slaying of the paschal lamb on the day before, or with the actual day of the Passover. The association with the Passover was therefore essential to Mark's understanding of the events of the last week.

The Passover

This is how the institution of the Passover is described in Exodus 12:1–15:

> The Lord said to Moses and Aaron in Egypt, 'This month is to be for you the first month, the first month of your year. Tell the whole community of Israel that on the tenth day of this month each man is to take a lamb for his family, one for each household.

If any household is too small for a whole lamb, they must share one with their nearest neighbour, having taken into account the number of people there are. You are to determine the amount of lamb needed in accordance with what each person will eat. The animals you choose must be year-old males without defect, and you may take them from the sheep or the goats. Take care of them until the fourteenth day of the month, when all the people of the community of Israel must slaughter them at twilight. Then they are to take some of the blood and put it on the sides and tops of the door-frames of the houses where they eat the lambs. That same night they are to eat the meat roasted over the fire, along with bitter herbs, and bread made without yeast. Do not eat the meat raw or cooked in water, but roast it over the fire – head, legs and inner parts. Do not leave any of it till morning; if some is left till morning, you must burn it. This is how you are to eat it: with your cloak tucked into your belt, your sandals on your feet and your staff in your hand. Eat it in haste; it is the Lord's Passover.

On that same night I will pass through Egypt and strike down every firstborn – both men and animals – and I will bring judgment on all the gods of Egypt. I am the Lord. The blood will be a sign for you on the houses where you are; and when I see the blood, I will pass over you. No destructive plague will touch you when I strike Egypt.

This is a day you are to commemorate; for the generations to come you shall celebrate it as a festival to the Lord – a lasting ordinance. For seven days you are to eat bread made without yeast. On the first day remove the yeast from your houses, for whoever eats anything with yeast in it from the first day until the seventh must be cut off from Israel'.

I need not bother the reader with the innumerable discussions that have taken place in Old Testament circles about the significance of this narrative. All I need to say is that it would have been accepted at its face value by those who heard it read at the Passover celebrations. A scholar of the ancient world, Theophilus (late second century AD) makes the point in commenting on the last supper that it would not appear that Jesus and his disciples ate it 'with their cloaks tucked into their belts, with their sandals on their feet and a staff in their hand' (12:11 above). But then, of course, the practice had changed over the years. By the time of Jesus it was no longer a domestic or tribal ceremony. It had become a great festival day, the greatest in the Jewish calendar, and from all over the world pilgrims poured into Jerusalem to join in the Temple services.

Circumstances do change the form and meaning of ecclesiastical rites. For example, we might have supposed that the Christians would have celebrated the Eucharist on a Thursday evening rather than on a Sunday morning if they had wished to be true to its historical origins, but many of the early Christians were slaves, and so it became the practice to celebrate the last supper not on Thursday evening but on Sunday morning, the day of resurrection, before the day's work began. So I am afraid that Theophilus's observation does not help us to decide whether the last supper was, or was not, a Passover meal. But in any case the Jewish Passover would have dominated the minds of Jesus and his disciples. They were Jews and the Passover would have meant everything to them.

It is a point well made by Jeremiah Unterman, associate professor of Jewish studies at Barry University, Florida, in his contribution to *Harper's Bible Dictionary*, that:

> The traditions of God's love and of His saving acts prompted the nascent Christian community, according to the gospels at the command of Jesus, to celebrate a thanksgiving festival commemorating the Passover he celebrated with his disciples the night before his crucifixion. The centrality of that observance for the Christian faith, drawing on the Passover as the central observance for the Jewish faith, clearly shows how deeply-rooted Christianity is in the historic life and faith of the people of Israel. (p. 754)

Mark himself would have applauded that judgment. The betrayal, last supper, crucifixion and the resurrection can only be understood in the context of the miraculous deliverance of Israel from Egypt, and the subsequent history of the chosen people. Whatever else Jesus may or may not have been, he was 'the Lamb of God, who takes away the sin of the world' (John 1:29). Mark would have learnt that lesson, if from no other, from St Paul – 'For Christ, our Passover lamb, has been sacrificed' (1 Cor. 5:7).

Why did Judas betray Jesus?

It is easy to see why the association between Jesus's death and the Passover has dominated the theology of the death of Christ, but does it throw any light on the treachery of Judas? Mark's gospel is dominated, as we have seen, by the conception of the 'Messianic secret' or, perhaps more accurately, the 'hidden Messiah'. The reaction of contemporary Judaism to Jesus was ambivalent. Even John the Baptist, the greatest of prophets, acknowledged as such by Jesus, had occasion to send a message to him, asking directly whether or not he was the Messiah (Matt. 11:3). Jesus replied:

> Go back and report to John what you hear and see. The blind receive sight, the lame walk, those who have leprosy are cured, the deaf hear, the dead are raised, and the good news is preached to the poor. Blessed is the man who does not fall away on account of me. (Matt. 11:4–6)

Jesus's disciples, some of whom – if John's gospel is to be believed – had been followers of John the Baptist, had similar doubts. Right to the end they were still harbouring old-fashioned Messianic hopes of a conquering Messiah who would put the Romans to flight and establish Israel in their place. When Peter said at Caesarea Philippi, 'You are the Christ' he was still not wholly disabused of his old ideas about the Messiah. That is why he rebuked Jesus for even suggesting that he was to suffer and die at the hands of his people.

If even the disciples were still in the grip of the past, the rulers of Israel and the teachers of the Law could be forgiven for failing to abandon the conventional expectation of a warlike, conquering Messiah. It was Judas's tragic destiny to embody in himself all the more fanatical and reactionary instincts of his race. While the other disciples stumbled towards some dim understanding of Jesus's true role in the world, Judas remained entrenched in his own unchanging hope of the old nationalistic Messiah.

It is no accident that Judas was a Judean, a man of Kerioth, a village in southern Judea, referred to in Joshua 15:25 and Jeremiah 48:24. He may well have despised those crude Galileans whom Jesus had chosen for his other disciples. Perhaps he was always a man apart from the others, indulging his own fantasies, nursing his own convictions. John asserts that Judas was a thief (John 12:6). But Mark does not say so. He may be pointing to the nature of his treachery when he associated Judas's decision to go to the high priest with the anointing at Bethany.

This was the last straw. Here is a man, to whom he had honestly given his life, welcoming this useless gesture by an unknown woman in the house of Simon the Leper. Was this the moment of glory for which Judas and the Jews had long waited, when the Son of Man would come on the clouds and his angels with him, to establish his authority on earth for ever? Was this little domestic incident in the house of a leper the culmination of trembling years of hope and expectation, of struggle and suffering, of captivity and exile? The slow process of disclosure, which was beginning to bear fruit in the minds of his other disciples, was lost on Judas. He felt 'betrayed'. This kind of Messiah was not for him.

In Mark's mind, the treachery of Judas is a symbol of the treachery of Judaism as a whole in its stubborn refusal to recognise the 'hidden Messiah'. Jerusalem, 'you who kill the prophets and stone those sent to you' (Matt. 23:37). And now the holy city would compound its wickedness and kill the Lord of life. Judas committed suicide. The proud men who sat in Moses' seat, unworthy representatives of a great world religion, committed suicide, too. They plotted and contrived the death of the Messiah. In less than forty years there was no Moses' seat in which to sit. The judgment of God had been passed on that 'unbelieving and perverse generation' (Matt. 17:17).

The young man in the garden

The passage we have been considering ends on a curious note – the story of a young man who fled naked from the scene in

Gethsemane. Many and various are the explanations which
have been offered for this incident. The fact that it is omitted
both from Matthew and from Luke suggests that they did not
understand it either. There are, I believe, solid grounds for
believing, with many a modern commentator, that it is a
reference to Mark himself. We know that his mother's home
was in Jerusalem; it is possible that the last supper was held
there, and some commentators have gone so far as to suggest
that he followed Jesus and his disciples when they left the
house, or that he had wind of the plot to arrest Jesus, but
arrived in the garden just too late to warn him.

Any such reconstructions will, of course, always be precarious. But if there is any truth in it, then we can see why
Mark included the incident and Matthew and Luke omitted it.
For him it is a kind of signature in the corner of the canvas he
has been painting. But even if the young man was not Mark
himself, the incident remains highly evocative, and has all the
marks of an eye-witness account.

It is an odd quirk of the human mind to remember a
singularly trivial happening in the midst of acute danger or
painful confusion. The garden was full of noise and disturbance. The disciples were stunned by the appearance of one of
their number on the side of their enemies. They heard their
Master's calm and magisterial rebuke to the crowd. They
were in a state of panic and confusion. Yet, one of them,
apparently to his dying day, remembered that glimpse of the
young man fleeing naked from the garden.

There is a sense in which these two, seemingly irrelevant,
verses take us back to the origins of the Christian faith. We
feel the human emotions flooding through the sparse narrative. We stand once more where Jesus and the apostles stood.
We feel the tension and the alarm and the sense of doom
which has descended upon them. We have not walked in
Gethsemane, but we share the agony of the Messiah as he
faces up, for the last time but not for the first time, to the
appalling suffering that lies only a few hours ahead. It was 'the
agony of the whole world pumped through the channels of a
single heart'. We sense the feeling of shame which must have
flowed through the minds of the disciples over and over again

as they recalled their gross lack of sympathy for Jesus in his ordeal.

They will remember the futility of an impulsive act of violence when the Lord of all the earth could have summoned legions of angels to his help if he had so desired. We share with them, for we have known it in ourselves, that experience of collapse and flight in the face of the enemy. The Garden of Gethsemane is not just a place on the map. It is the scenery against which many an act of human folly, violence and shame is enacted over and over again. We flee from it, trembling and naked.

16

CAIAPHAS

[Mark 14:53–65]

[53] They took Jesus to the high priest, and all the chief priests, elders and teachers of the law came together. [54] Peter followed him at a distance, right into the courtyard of the high priest. There he sat with the guards and warmed himself at the fire.

[55] The chief priests and the whole Sanhedrin were looking for evidence against Jesus so that they could put him to death, but they did not find any. [56] Many testified falsely against him, but their statements did not agree.

[57] Then some stood up and gave this false testimony against him: [58] "We heard him say, 'I will destroy this man-made temple and in three days will build another, not made by man.'" [59] Yet even then their testimony did not agree.

[60] Then the high priest stood up before them and asked Jesus, "Are you not going to answer? What is this testimony that these men are bringing against you?" [61] But Jesus remained silent and gave no answer.

Again the high priest asked him, "Are you the Christ, the Son of the Blessed One?"

[62] "I am," said Jesus. "And you will see the Son of Man sitting at the right hand of the Mighty One and coming on the clouds of heaven."

[63] The high priest tore his clothes. "Why do we need any more witnesses?" he asked. [64] "You have heard the blasphemy. What do you think?"

They all condemned him as worthy of death. [65] Then some began to spit at him; they blindfolded him, struck him with their fists, and said, "Prophesy!" And the guards took him and beat him.

Paul wrote his 'letter to the Romans' some ten years before the likely date of Mark's gospel. The tone and content of the letter suggest that the congregation there was composed largely of Gentiles, but with a small cohesive group of Christian Jews among them. This would explain the reference to the dietary laws (Rom. 14:19–23) which often proved a source of division in the Church (Acts 15). It would account for his command that they should accept each other (Rom. 15:7), and it would make his long sections on the status of the Jews intelligible (Rom. 2:17–3:31; 9:1–11:32). It would also explain his insistence on the fact that the Gentile Christians were no less the objects of God's love than their Jewish brothers. They were all, Gentile and Jewish Christians, 'sons of Abraham', justified as he was by faith in the living God (Rom. 15:7–12; 4:16).

The Congregation in Rome

It is unlikely that the congregation at Rome would have changed much in the intervening years, though the Jewish element in it may have been strengthened by the return of the Jews to Rome in AD 64 after their previous banishment. Both to the Jewish and Gentile members of the Church the arrest and trial of Jesus would have seemed of the greatest importance. Why had the rulers of Israel conspired against their own Messiah? The answer to that question emerges elsewhere in the gospel. But the other question which would particularly have worried the Jewish members arises in the account of the trial, during which the witnesses asserted that they had heard Jesus say that he would 'destroy this man-made temple and in three days will build another, not made by man' (Mark 14:58).

Jewish Christians in Palestine might still be in the habit of attending the Temple (Acts 2:46), and it is possible that even Jewish Christians in Rome still made the pilgrimage to Jerusalem for the feasts. All over the diaspora loyal Jews still kept their windows open towards Jerusalem for the hours of prayer (Dan. 6:10). Did Jesus really say that he would destroy this sacred building, the repository of centuries of Jewish tradition, the joy of the whole earth and particularly of the sons of Abraham whom Melchizedek, the priest of God most high, had blessed on that very site (Gen. 14:18–20)?

The Temple Saying

The saying about the Temple, attributed to Jesus, remains every bit as difficult as it must have seemed to the first readers or hearers of the gospel. The saying, or something like it, seems to be integral to the New Testament tradition. Matthew qualifies the Marcan version slightly when he reports that the witnesses testified only that Jesus said, 'I am able to destroy the temple of God and rebuild it in three days' (Matt. 26:61).

To show how persistent the tradition was, one has only to turn to the Acts of the Apostles where the witnesses against Stephen said, 'This fellow never stops speaking against this holy place and against the law. For we have heard him say that this Jesus of Nazareth will destroy this place and will change the customs Moses handed down to us' (Acts 6:13–14). And it appears in the apocryphal gospel of Thomas. It takes a slightly different form: 'I shall destroy this house and no one will be able to rebuild it.' It does not appear in Luke's account of the evidence against Jesus, but it is known to John, who records it in association with the cleansing of the Temple, where in response to the objections of the Jews, Jesus said:

> Destroy this temple, and I will raise it again in three days. The Jews replied, 'It has taken forty-six years to build this temple and you are going to raise it in three days?' But he spoke of the temple of his body. After he was raised from the dead, his disciples recalled what he had said. Then they believed the Scripture and the words which Jesus had spoken. (John 2:19–22)

It appears therefore that Jesus really did say something like this, though it may have been quoted out of context by the false witnesses, and the Jewish members of the congregation at Rome would have had to come to terms with it. The great Temple in Jerusalem had indeed become a den of thieves,

and had forfeited God's protection. Within a few years the
message had been spelled out in blood and fire when the city
fell to the Roman armies.

Luke and John

For the moment we must leave the congregation in Rome
with their problems, and turn back to Jerusalem, to the high
priest's house on the Thursday evening following the arrest of
Jesus in the Garden of Gethsemane. On this point, at least,
the four evangelists agree – when Jesus was arrested he was
taken to the high priest's house, but there are significant
variations of detail and it is important to know what they
are.

Matthew follows Mark closely. In Luke's account the only
thing that happens in the high priest's house is that the men
who were guarding Jesus began mocking and beating him.
They blindfolded him and demanded: '"Prophesy! Who hit
you?" and they said many other insulting things to him' (Luke
22:63–65).

No conversation with Caiaphas at that point is recorded
but the following morning Jesus is brought before the council
of the elders of the people, both the chief priests and the
teachers of the Law, who ask him one question: 'If you are the
Christ, tell us' (Luke 22:67). This is followed by a further
question – 'Are you then the Son of God?' Jesus replied, 'You
are right in saying I am.' Then they said, 'Why do we need
any more testimony? We have heard it from his own lips.'
(vv. 70–1).

In John, after his arrest Jesus was taken not to the house of
Caiaphas but to Annas, who was the father-in-law of
Caiaphas. There he was questioned about his disciples and his
teaching (John 18:19). Jesus replied:

> I have spoken openly to the world . . . I always taught in
> synagogues or at the temple, where all the Jews come together.
> said nothing in secret. Why question me? Ask those who heard
> me. Surely they know what I said. (John 18:20–1)

This was regarded by one of the officials as an impertinence to
Annas, and he struck Jesus on the face. From there Jesus was
sent to Caiaphas and, without any account of what happened
in the presence of Caiaphas, he was taken early in the
morning to Pilate. John therefore does not record any trial
before a Jewish court, only an informal examination by
Annas. Mark and Matthew thus stand for one tradition, Luke
stands for a second, John for a third.

This ought not to surprise us, because the evangelists would
be relying entirely on hearsay evidence; according to the
Synoptists Peter was the only disciple anywhere near the
action, but he certainly would not have been in any position
to know precisely what happened in the house of Annas or
subsequently at the High Priest's palace. Such information as
the evangelists had could only have been derived from members of the Sanhedrin who subsequently believed and became
members of the Church, e.g. Joseph of Arimathea, or
Nicodemus. But even they would not have been present at the
informal examination before Annas, and may not have been
present at all at the meeting of the Sanhedrin, especially if it
was summoned in haste at night. There were seventy or so
members of the Sanhedrin, but a quorum of twenty-three was
sufficient for business to be conducted. We turn, therefore, to
the earliest account we have, that is Mark's, in the knowledge
that any reconstruction of the events of that evening are
bound to be hypothetical, and incapable of documentary
proof.

Mark

The most serious problem for the reader of Mark's gospel is to
know whether he intended us to believe that Jesus was
formally convicted of blasphemy by the Sanhedrin. If so, it
was a trial which broke every rule in the book. It was held at
night, apparently in the High Priest's house, and if Mark's
view of the day of the Passover is correct, it was held during
the most solemn festival of the Jewish year. The court
appeared to begin with an assumption of guilt, and positively

looked for witnesses who could testify to it. In a capital case of this kind there should in any case have been an adjournment of the Sanhedrin pending conviction at a second meeting. No judge or president of a court would have the right to insist on a reply which incriminated the accused.

But in any case Jesus's reply did not constitute the offence of blasphemy. It may not have been politic to claim to be the Messiah, but it was not blasphemous to do so in the strict legal sense. So I incline to the view, most recently propounded by Anthony Harvey in his book *Jesus and the Constraints of History* (Duckworth, 1982) that 'the intention of the evangelists was not to report a trial, but rather a meeting of the Jewish authorities to decide whether Jesus was to be handed over to Pilate'. This does not solve all the problems, but it would have eased the conscience of Mark's Jewish Christian readers, who would otherwise have seen the trial as a flagrant abuse of the Jewish Law, which they still held sacred.

Why refer the case to Pilate?

If this is a true reading of Mark's gospel, we have to ask the further question: Why did the Sanhedrin feel it necessary to hand over a member of their own race to the secular power? The most obvious answer to the question is the one given by John: 'It is not lawful for us to put any man to death' (John 18:31 RSV). But that answer does not wholly accord with Luke's account of a similar trial before the Sanhedrin described in Acts 6:8–7:60, where Stephen was brought before the Sanhedrin for 'blasphemy against Moses and against God' (Acts 6:11). Stephen received the normal penalty for such an offence and was stoned to death 'and Saul was there, giving approval to his death' (Acts 8:1).

The problem is part of the wider issue of the degree of self-government which the Jews enjoyed in the Roman empire in the first century. It is fully discussed in vol. I of *The Jewish People in the First Century* (Van Gorcum, 1974). But for all the detailed learning deployed on the issue, there is still no definitive answer. If the appearance of Jesus before the

Sanhedrin was not a formal trial but an enquiry, it might well be that the Sanhedrin preferred in this case not to exercise the rights they may have had, but to shed their responsibility and submit the case to the secular power.

It is known that the Jewish authorities in the first century were under obligation to refer any case involving 'a risk to public order' to the Roman procurator – and this may well have been the reasoning behind the decision of the Sanhedrin. The account of the informal enquiry shows how difficult it was going to be for the Sanhedrin to make any religious charges stick, whereas, in their view, the actions of Jesus in the cleansing of the Temple could have constituted a 'risk to public order'. Furthermore, it delivered the Jewish authorities from the invidious task of executing one who had a strong popular following and was viewed by some as the expected Messiah.

Moreover, at a full meeting of the Sanhedrin, held in accordance with legal procedures, violent differences of opinion might well have surfaced between those who did and those who did not favour action against Jesus. When, on a later occasion, Peter and John appeared before the Sanhedrin the council had to be content with threatening them because: 'They could not decide how to punish them, because all the people were praising God for what had happened' (Acts 4:21). The implications of this decision to submit the case to Pilate begin to emerge in the next chapter.

Caiaphas

It is interesting that nowhere in his gospel does Mark actually mention the name of Caiaphas, although he figures prominently in the 'demonology' of the early Church. It could be, of course, that Mark had little knowledge of him, writing at a distance of some forty years from the event, and ten years at least after the death of Caiaphas. It was just Caiaphas's misfortune to be in office for this particular period, and to bear the odium of the decision he was called to make. It could easily have been otherwise, in which case Caiaphas would have gone down in history as a minor figure in the annals of Judaism among many of the other High Priests who held office in the early part of the first century.

Josephus tells us that between the accession of Herod the Great in 37 BC and the destruction of the Temple in AD 70 twenty-eight High Priests held office, mostly at the whim of King Herod himself, or subsequently of the Roman authorities. Furthermore, Caiaphas might never have held office at all if he had not married the daughter of Annas, founder of an ecclesiastical dynasty which provided eight High Priests in the period with which we are concerned. There is no proof that Caiaphas actually purchased the office, as many of the high priests did, but it is certain that he owed his elevation to the prestige of the house of Annas to which he had been admitted by marriage.

His position, therefore, as president of the Sanhedrin, was particularly perilous. He no doubt had rivals within the Sanhedrin itself who resented his promotion, and would have relished his embarrassment. He had a father-in-law who had all the strings of power in his own hands, and would no doubt be quick to remind his son-in-law to whom he owed his office. And he was responsible, as the ecclesiastical and political head of worldwide Judaism, for maintaining the fragile status quo with the emperor in Rome, and his representative in Palestine.

It was Caiaphas, according to John 18:14 (RSV), who 'had given counsel to the Jews that it was expedient that one man should die for the people'. As he saw it, he was weighing the future of worldwide Judaism against the fate of a single individual of no apparent consequence, whose activities threatened the status quo. If there had been a riot at the Passover, Caiaphas would have found himself in deep trouble with the state for not taking precautions against it. No doubt he would gladly have rid himself of his responsibility, but there was no way he could do so. So he, perhaps more than any other member of the Sanhedrin, was desperate to find a charge against Jesus which would 'stand up' in a Roman court.

When the witnesses failed, he had to resort to desperate

measures, and demanded under oath that Jesus should declare whether or not he was the Messiah. The unambiguous answer which Jesus gave was all that he needed, not to procure the death penalty under Jewish Law, but to be able to hand him over to Pilate as a rival 'king' of the Jews. By now Caiaphas had lost all sense of proportion: he was in no position even to consider whether Jesus was or was not the expected Messiah. Nothing else mattered at this moment but that this 'troubler of Israel' should be safely put away and the High Priest once more be free to be the High Priest, presiding over the Temple, receiving the acclamations of the people as he ministered in the holy place, regarded with awe and reverence as the indispensable guardian of correct ritual and sound doctrine.

We must not be too hard on Caiaphas. Perhaps Mark deliberately chose not to mention his name because essentially it was his office that was at fault. Probably no other High Priest in the latter days of the Temple would have done any better. He was trapped in the machinery of government and by most standards – political and ecclesiastical – he did the only possible thing. The Jewish hierarchy of that day was no more blameworthy than the Christian hierarchy has been since, often sacrificing truth to profit, justice to political expediency, the freedom of the man of God to the supposed 'good of the Church'.

Of Judas Jesus said: 'It were better for him that he had never been born'. Of Caiaphas he might have said it would have been better for him if he had never been made high priest to bear the awesome responsibility of this particular day and to stand condemned for ever at the bar of history. We must not be too hard on Caiaphas. Many a 'high priest' in the history of Christendom has succumbed to the temptation and pressures of his office, thereby 'crucifying the Son of God afresh'.

17

PONTIUS PILATE

[Mark 15:1–15]

15 Very early in the morning, the chief priests, with the elders, the teachers of the law and the whole Sanhedrin, reached a decision. They bound Jesus, led him away and turned him over to Pilate.

[2] "Are you the king of the Jews?" asked Pilate.

"Yes, it is as you say," Jesus replied.

[3] The chief priests accused him of many things. [4] So again Pilate asked him, "Aren't you going to answer? See how many things they are accusing you of."

[5] But Jesus still made no reply, and Pilate was amazed.

[6] Now it was the custom at the Feast to release a prisoner whom the people requested. [7] A man called Barabbas was in prison with the insurrectionists who had committed murder in the uprising. [8] The crowd came up and asked Pilate to do for them what he usually did.

[9] "Do you want me to release to you the king of the Jews?" asked Pilate, [10] knowing it was out of envy that the chief priests had handed Jesus over to him. [11] But the chief priests stirred up the crowd to have Pilate release Barabbas instead.

[12] "What shall I do, then, with the one you call the king of the Jews?" Pilate asked them.

[13] "Crucify him!" they shouted.

[14] "Why? What crime has he committed?" asked Pilate.

But they shouted all the louder, "Crucify him!"

[15] Wanting to satisfy the crowd, Pilate released Barabbas to them. He had Jesus flogged, and handed him over to be crucified.

The 'trial' before the Sanhedrin had elicited from Jesus the first plain assertion that he was indeed the Messiah. According to Mark, Jesus himself had known it from the time of his baptism. He had heard a voice from heaven saying, 'You are my son whom I love; with you I am well pleased' (Mark 1:11). The secret of his being had been vouchsafed in part to Peter in his great confession of faith at Caesarea Philippi. 'You are the Christ,' he had said (Mark 8:29). Blind Bartimaeus had hailed him as 'Son of David' (Mark 10:47). For those with eyes to see, it was as Messiah that he exercised his right to purify the Temple. He had been anointed with oil at a secret coronation in the house of Simon the Leper. Otherwise the 'Messianic secret' had been well kept, in accordance with his instructions to his followers. But at his trial in response to the high priest's adjuration he had himself breached the secret. At last he had responded to the demand of the Jews reported in John 10:24 – 'How long will you keep us in suspense? If you are the Christ, tell us plainly.'

The irony would not have been lost upon Mark that, when he did tell the official representatives of the people that he was indeed the Messiah, they wholly ignored the claim. They did not even discuss it in the Sanhedrin. All that mattered to Caiaphas was that he had now obtained an admission which would enable him to invoke the secular power and to achieve the end upon which he had set his heart. In his mind anyone who claimed to be the Messiah must be an imposter – which was a strange attitude in the official representative of a race which had persistently, through thick and thin, through war and exile, clung to the hope of the coming Messiah. It is, I fear, the danger of any official religion well-entrenched in its own traditions and well-adjusted to the world to treat any 'Messiah' as an imposter. There was already too much at stake for Caiaphas to take Jesus's claim seriously.

So, having achieved its aim, the delegation of the San-hedrin 'led Jesus away and turned him over to Pilate'. It is difficult to say whether or not Mark regarded this early morning meeting as a formal ratification of a decision already reached, but, either way, he is at pains to emphasise that it was the official leaders of Judaism who were responsible for handing Jesus over to the Roman authority. Whether it was a formal 'trial' or a hearing or an examination, it was riddled with irregularities, and the Sanhedrin had failed to establish any guilt for which the prisoner could justly have been condemned. They were intent only on finding a cause which would stand up in a Roman court and it was with this cause that they now hastened with their prisoner to Pilate.

The night before

Before we turn to the trial before Pilate there is a preliminary question which we must ask. How was it that Pilate 'very early in the morning' was prepared to hold an emergency court? He was no lover of the Jewish people, as will be evident from the account of his career, and he would not normally have put himself out to accommodate them.

At this point we must retrace our steps to the upper room and the Garden of Gethsemane. The last supper would probably have started at sundown, whether it was a Passover meal or the anticipation of the Passover. We know that Judas left before the supper ended, say at about 7.00 p.m. (by our reckoning). The house of Caiaphas was not more than a hundred yards from the supposed site of the upper room, and it would have taken Judas only a minute or two to accomplish his purpose. So let us suppose that the supper ended at about 8.00 p.m. Jesus and his disciples traversed the city and took the road to Bethany which would have passed the Garden of Gethsemane. It is a matter of only a mile and a half, and Jesus could have been in the garden well before 9.00 p.m. The detachment sent to arrest Jesus, if they were the Temple police and started from the Temple precinct, would have taken less than half an hour to reach the garden.

But Mark's narrative gives the impression of a long wait in the garden before the detachment arrived, long enough any way for the disciples to fall asleep three times, long enough too, for Jesus's long struggle with himself before submitting to the will of his Father. There seems, therefore, to have been a considerable delay between the time that Caiaphas received Judas's message and the departure of the detachment from the Temple – and this when speed was of the essence of the matter if the Jewish authorities were not to lose the opportunity of arresting Jesus before, as they must have supposed, he continued on the road to Bethany and his night's lodging. The delay is only explicable if there were some things which Caiaphas had to do before he could commit himself to the arrest. He may well have had to make sure that a quorum of the Sanhedrin would be available at that hour of night. He may have wished to have witnesses at hand who could provide the necessary evidence upon which a judgment could be reached. But above all it was essential that Pilate could be available in the early morning for what Caiaphas hoped would prove to be the mere formality of a trial.

The only way to achieve that end before the days of the telephone was for Caiaphas to visit Pilate in Herod's palace, which the governor was accustomed to use when he stayed in Jerusalem. It would have been less than half a mile, but it would all have taken time, and there was no point in ordering the Temple guard out unless he could be sure of Pilate's compliance. Given Pilate's character, such compliance may not easily have been achieved – but perhaps the fate of this itinerant preacher from Galilee would not have seemed sufficiently important for the governor to resist Jewish wishes. (For an interesting and thorough reconstruction of the night before the trial see Morison, *Who Moved the Stone?* (Faber and Faber, 1943).)

Pontius Pilate

'Given Pilate's character'. What do we know about this man, who held in his hands for a few moments on a cold Friday morning the fate of all humanity? Herod the Great had died in 4 BC and one of his sons, Archelaus, was appointed as Ethnarch of Judea in his place. He proved a headstrong, unreliable ally of Rome and was deposed in AD 6. From that time Judaea came under the direct control of the emperor, who ruled it through a series of so-called 'procurators'. Such colonial appointments tended to be of short duration. In less than a hundred years there were nineteen procurators of

Judea. Pontius Pilate held the office for an exceptionally long time, from AD 26–36, and for the whole of this time he worked with Caiaphas as his religious counterpart.

There had to be a great deal of collusion between them, and the fact that they both held office for so long suggests that a useful balance had been struck between the demands of Roman government and the susceptibilities of the Jewish people. But Pilate had his disasters, as well might any procurator in that troubled province. Josephus speaks about his cruelty and oppression. Philo quotes a letter from Agrippa to Caligula which speaks of him as 'inflexible, merciless and obstinate'. For example, on his first visit from Caesarea to Jerusalem he insisted on bringing into the city the military standards of his troops, and grossly offended Jewish opinion which regarded the standards as idolatrous. It caused a riot in Caesarea. Pilate was forced to yield.

As if that were not enough, he then placed golden shields with the emperor's name on them in his residence in Jerusalem: on that occasion the emperor had to intervene personally to see that they were removed. Then, in a well-intentioned attempt to introduce extra water supplies into Jerusalem, he appropriated a Temple fund to build an aqueduct. This no doubt seemed sensible to a career civil servant in the Roman bureaucracy, but to the Jews it was a gross misuse of Temple funds. Many were injured and killed in the ensuing riot. Luke describes how Pilate had mingled the blood of Galileans with their sacrifices (Luke 13:1) and Josephus says that it was the slaughter of the Samaritans in AD 35 which caused the emperor to lose patience and to withdraw him from the province.

We have, of course, to allow for the animus which any subject people may feel towards the representative of a foreign power, and if he was as bad as Jewish sources tend to suggest, it is surprising that he should have survived in his office for ten years in a province which had been the graveyard of many ambitious officials before him. But it has been suggested that his long tenure of office may have been due, not so much to his own virtue, as to the fact that he was married to a certain Claudia Procula, who was reputed to

be the illegitimate daughter of Claudia, the third wife of
Tiberius. It could be that he was saved from his follies by his
influence at court.

Nevertheless, with the reputation he had already earned he
would need to mollify the Jewish authorities whenever he
could safely do so. When Caiaphas approached him, therefore, on the Thursday evening, with the news that there was
a certain 'malefactor' from Galilee who had been causing
trouble in Herod Antipas's territory and had now come to
Jerusalem with a large following of excited disciples, Pilate
had to listen. When he heard that the Jewish authorities were
proposing to arrest the 'malefactor' later that night, he could
hardly have objected, and when Caiaphas told him of their
plan to hold a meeting of the Sanhedrin overnight, and that
they would bring the prisoner to Pilate in the early morning,
he was reluctant to refuse.

He did not pretend to understand the devious mind of
Caiaphas and he was no doubt on the alert for yet another
bit of sharp practice. But no Roman governor could be
indifferent to the story, however garbled, of a prophet arriving from troublesome Galilee at the head of an excited band
of followers, especially on the eve of the Passover, when there
would be tens of thousands of Jewish pilgrims in the city.
Roman justice was real but rough, and especially rough at any
threat to the imperial domination of a conquered province.
The previous career of Pilate, his political situation and his
violent temperament, are essential information for our
understanding of what occurred very early the next morning.

The trial

If the previous evening followed the course which I have
suggested, then the outcome of the trial on the following
morning was a foregone conclusion. By colluding with the
Sanhedrin and agreeing to an emergency court Pilate left
himself little room for manoeuvre. He was sufficiently a man
of the world to know that Caiaphas was not concerned for the
safety of the empire; he knew that 'it was out of envy the Chief

Priests had handed Jesus over to him'. Yet there was obviously something about the presence of Jesus which troubled him, and for all his hard-headedness and political concern, he hesitated to fulfil the contract which in a sense he had all but signed the night before.

The gospel accounts of the trial all reflect that hesitation, although they differ substantially from each other in their presentation of the events. Matthew records that Pilate's wife sent him a message – 'Don't have anything to do with that innocent man, for I have suffered a great deal today in a dream because of him' (Matt. 27:19) – a message which could only have deepened Pilate's anxiety. Luke records how eagerly Pilate seized on the information that Jesus was a Galilean and sent him off to Herod, who happened to be in Jerusalem at the time. Luke displays a wry sense of humour when he says 'on that day Herod and Pilate became friends; before this they had been enemies' (Luke 23:6–12). John does not record any 'trial' by the Sanhedrin at all – only a brief examination by Annas (John 18:19–24).

Such trial as Jesus had was before Pilate, and John's record is fuller and more circumstantial than any of the others. Pilate asks what the charges are, to which the delegation from the Sanhedrin replies, 'If he were not a criminal . . . we would not have handed him over to you' (John 18:30), a reply which does indeed suggest a previous arrangement with Pilate which he now seems to deny. Pilate, now eager to unload the responsibility of what is proving to be a troublesome issue, resorts to the obvious tactic: 'Take him yourselves and judge him by your own law' (John 18:31). Gallio, the proconsul of Achaea, uses the same device when Paul is brought before him by his Jewish opponents:

> If you Jews were making a complaint about some misdemeanour or serious crime, it would be reasonable for me to listen to you. But since it involves questions about words and names and your own law – settle the matter yourselves. I will not be a judge of such things. (Acts 18:14–15)

The gospels are united, therefore, in suggesting that Pilate made strenuous efforts to release Jesus, or at least to avoid the responsibility for convicting him. He even went so far as to invoke a custom, which he had himself introduced during his procuratorship, of releasing at the Passover any prisoner whom the Jewish authorities desired to be released. The custom had obviously been intended as a conciliatory gesture towards a people who were notoriously difficult to govern. But, here again, Pilate was thwarted. It is possible that the people who were present that morning outside the praetorium had come for the very purpose of exercising their right in asking for a prisoner. Whether for that reason or whether, as Mark suggests, it was the chief priests who stirred up the crowd, the people asked Pilate to release Barabbas, who had committed murder in the course of a recent insurrection.

It is an interesting observation that in some versions of Matthew's gospel the full name of Barabbas is given as 'Jesus Barabbas'. The name Jesus (in the Hebrew, 'Joshua') was a very common name in the first century, and if the variant text is right it would suggest that the crowd was moved not so much by malice as by confusion about the offer that was being made to them.

Be that as it may, it was Pilate's last throw. The specific charge as recorded by Luke was that: 'We [the Sanhedrin] have found this man subverting our nation. He opposes payment of taxes to Caesar and claims to be Christ, a king' (Luke 23:2). This was a grossly false charge, but once it had been laid it would have been a very brave colonial officer who did not act upon it. The die was cast. No formal conviction is recorded; the gospels simply say that Pilate handed him over to be crucified.

The trial and the early Church

The implications of this 'trial' narrative are of great importance to the early Church. The gospels vary from each other in detail, but they are united on the following points. The first is that Jesus is convicted on the evidence that he was 'king of the Jews'. It was to be as the Messiah, so Christians believed, that Jesus went to the cross. It was as an imposter, so the Jewish leaders believed, that he went to the cross. This was to be the source of bitter conflict between the two communities in the centuries that lay ahead. This is a crucial and inescapable divergence of view: it is the crux of the argument.

The second point is that which is suggested by the gospel narratives throughout. John records that Pilate actually said to the Jews, 'Look, I am bringing him out to you to let you know that I find no basis for a charge against him' (John 19:4). And the point is reiterated when, at verse 12, it is said that 'Pilate tried to set Jesus free, but the Jews kept shouting, "If you let this man go you are no friend of Caesar."' The implication is clear that it was the Jewish authorities who were responsible for the death of Jesus on a false charge which the Roman governor had perceived to be false. Roman law in the person of Pilate had declared Jesus innocent. This was an important point to make at a time when Christians and Jews were in varying degrees subject to persecution by the Roman authorities. It helped to mark off the Christians as a distinct community whose founder was no threat to the empire, and who had been formally acquitted by a Roman judge.

The third point is a theological one. It has sometimes been observed in recent scholarship how often the Greek word for 'deliver' or 'hand over' is used in the Passion narratives. In St Mark's narrative, for example, it occurs ten times, and it is no accident. Judas betrayed or handed over Jesus to the High Priests. The High Priests delivered or handed over Jesus to Pilate. Pilate delivers or hands over Jesus to crucifixion. It is recognised that in Mark's gospel the figure of the 'suffering servant' of Isaiah is never far from his mind, and it is particularly interesting, therefore, that the Greek version of Isaiah 53:12, which is probably the version with which Mark was familiar, reads as follows: 'He bore the sins of many and was delivered because of their iniquities.' It would be difficult to exaggerate the importance of Isaiah 53 to the later understanding of Jesus's Passion and death, and it is one sentence in that passage that lies at the heart of our understanding: 'Yet it was the will of the Lord to bruise him' (Isaiah 53:10 RSV).

So Mark is suggesting that Judas, the High Priests and Pilate were not acting entirely of their own volition, out of greed or envy or expediency: they were the unwitting agents of God himself for the ultimate salvation of the world. This is the plain, if mysterious, message of the gospel. Jesus himself endorsed it in his threefold prediction of his coming Passion after the Transfiguration.

At any point Jesus could have avoided the fate which ultimately befell him. He need not have tangled with the Pharisees, who might otherwise have supported him in the Sanhedrin. He need not have gone up to Jerusalem at all. He could have kept a low profile and avoided a confrontation with the High Priests in the cleansing of the Temple. He could have excluded Judas altogether from his company. He need not have tarried in the Garden of Gethsemane; every instinct for personal safety would have urged him to go back to Bethany. But he kept to his course, believing that it was his life's vocation to suffer at the hands of men. He would have been familiar with Isaiah 53, and he would have known the verse which says – 'he shall see the fruit of the travail of his soul and shall be satisfied' (Isa. 53:11 RSV). Peter boldly expresses this conviction of the early Church when on the day of Pentecost he says:

> Men of Israel, listen to this: Jesus of Nazareth was a man accredited by God to you by miracles, wonders and signs, which God did among you through him, as you yourselves know. This man was handed over to you by God's set purpose and fore-knowledge; and you, with the help of wicked men, put him to death by nailing him to the cross. (Acts 2:22–3)

In this mystery the disciples, Judas, the High Priests and Pilate would have been hopelessly lost, floundering amid circumstances none of them could control. It has to be said that theologians have been wrestling ever since to understand why it should have 'pleased the Lord to bruise him'. There is no easy answer; it is part of the mystery of our redemption, which Mark himself did not wholly understand.

18

SIMON OF CYRENE

[Mark 15:16–32]

¹⁶The soldiers led Jesus away into the palace (that is, the Praetorium) and called together the whole company of soldiers.

¹⁷They put a purple robe on him, then twisted together a crown of thorns and set it on him. ¹⁸And they began to call out to him, "Hail, king of the Jews!" ¹⁹Again and again they struck him on the head with a staff and spat on him. Falling on their knees, they paid homage to him. ²⁰And when they had mocked him, they took off the purple robe and put his own clothes on him. Then they led him out to crucify him.

²¹A certain man from Cyrene, Simon, the father of Alexander and Rufus, was passing by on his way in from the country, and they forced him to carry the cross. ²²They brought Jesus to the place called Golgotha (which means The Place of the Skull). ²³Then they offered him wine mixed with myrrh, but he did not take it. ²⁴And they crucified him. Dividing up his clothes, they cast lots to see what each would get.

²⁵It was the third hour when they crucified him. ²⁶The written notice of the charge against him read: THE KING OF THE JEWS. ²⁷They crucified two robbers with him, one on his right and one on his left. ²⁹Those who passed by hurled insults at him, shaking their heads and saying, "So! You who are going to destroy the temple and build it in three days, ³⁰come down from the cross and save yourself!"

³¹In the same way the chief priests and the teachers of the law mocked him among themselves. "He saved others," they say, "but he can't save himself! ³²Let this Christ, this King of Israel, come down now from the cross, that we may see and believe." Those crucified with him also heaped insults on him.

The encounters I have described so far are widely separated from each other in distance and in time. They stretch from Tyre and Sidon to Jericho, and from the very beginning of Jesus's ministry until the end. But now I find myself describing three encounters which occur on the same day and within half a mile of each other – and there are curious, if unintended, contrasts between them.

The life of Pilate is well documented in religious and secular history. We know, as we have seen already, a great deal about his career so far and something about the end of his career. He was recalled to Rome shortly after his mishandling of the Samaritan affair in AD 36, just six years after the crucifixion of Christ. He was saved from impeachment by the death of Tiberius. There is a tradition that he and his wife subsequently became Christians, but the more persistent tradition is that, for reasons at present unknown, he committed suicide.

So he occupies an important, if doleful, place in the history of the world. Day after day, week after week, year after year, his memory is celebrated in the creeds of the Christian Church. 'Jesus', we say, 'was crucified also for us under Pontius Pilate.' We know all we need to know about Pontius Pilate.

The next encounter is with one of whom we know almost nothing, who did not occupy an official position and whose career is not recorded. All that we know about Simon is that he had two sons – Alexander and Rufus – and that he was a native of Cyrene. I put it like that because we cannot be absolutely sure whether Mark intended us to understand that he was now resident in Palestine, or that he was one of a party from Cyrene who had come to worship as a pilgrim at the feast. We can be sure, however, that it was significant for Mark that the man who was chosen to carry the cross of Christ was a 'foreigner' from Africa.

The Diaspora

After the death of Alexander the Great, Egypt was ruled by the Ptolemies who enlarged their territory westwards to include what we now call Libya. Cyrene was one of a group of towns on the North African coast which had been settled with Jews and others who had served in the army – as a way of keeping the territory secure for the Ptolemaic dynasty. So, in Cyrene, there was a substantial population of Jews who, when the territory was conquered by Rome in AD 74, continued to enjoy a degree of independence and civil liberty. It is believed that some Jews grew rich and powerful on the strength of the wool trade for which Cyrenaica was famed.

On the whole Jews and Greeks had lived amicably together, but under the Romans it proved to be a turbulent province and a very serious war broke out in the time of Trajan between the Jewish and Greek populations. Perhaps this is the time to make the point which may not be obvious to some readers. From the time of the destruction of Jerusalem and the ensuing exile in 586 BC the diaspora, as it was called, became increasingly important in the total life of Judaism. Long before the time of Jesus far more Jews were living outside Judea than were living in it. It is estimated that by the beginning of the first century there were two and a half million Jews in Judea, over four million elsewhere. It is even possible that one-tenth of the whole population of the empire was Jewish (De Lange – *Atlas of the Jewish World*, 1984).

To a large part of Jewry, therefore, Judea would have seemed a remote corner of the empire which some of them had never visited and which was thought of primarily as a place for rare pilgrimage at one or other of the great feasts. Inevitably there grew up in the diaspora forms of religious observance and attitudes to the world which were very different from those which obtained in the homeland. Inevitably there were tensions between the diaspora Jews and the Jerusalem hierarchy, and Caiaphas would have been conscious of them. Pilate, too, would have been aware that he was not dealing simply with a small subject people in Palestine, but with a widespread and influential constituency present in all the cities of the empire, and not least in Rome itself.

When the Jewish revolt broke out in AD 66 the Foreign Office in Rome would no doubt have kept a wary eye open for repercussions throughout the empire. There was little doubt that the Roman legions would triumph over the rebels in Palestine, but it would have been a different matter if it had spread to other subject territories where the Jews were strong and well organised. Mark, therefore, as one who had travelled throughout the diaspora with Paul, would have been more aware of this dimension than many of his fellow-countrymen in Palestine.

It is often observed that in the providence of God, the great Roman roads, the comparative security of travel and a common language were of great assistance in the promulgation of the gospel throughout the civilised world. What is often less observed is the importance of the diaspora 'connection' which ensured that wherever Paul and other missionaries went they would find men and women of their own race, meeting regularly in the synagogues and enjoying a high degree of civil liberty, whose religion was not based upon Temple observance but upon a common study of the Scriptures and a fervent hope for the coming of the Messiah.

It was this network of Jewish communities throughout the empire which proved to be the springboard for Christian mission which ultimately conquered the empire itself. Paul is seldom recorded as addressing his gospel to an exclusively Gentile environment, and when he does so – in Athens – he wins only modest success (Acts 17:34). It was when he spoke to Jews (and Gentile proselytes) about the coming of the Messiah that he could be sure of a hearing, if perhaps not always of agreement. What Mark saw in the encounter with Simon of Cyrene was the world dimension of what happened that day in Jerusalem. As Paul himself said, 'it was not done in a corner' (Acts 26:26). It is against this world background that we now have to consider in detail the events described in the passage above.

The fulfilment of Scripture

Doubts still persist as to whether the trial before Pilate took place as we have supposed in Herod's palace or in the Fortress

Antonia, half a mile away on the corner of the Temple site. Mark betrays some uncertainty when he suggests that the soldiers in charge of Jesus called together the whole company or 'cohort' to take part in the fun. The cohort would have been stationed in the Fortress Antonia, and it was presumably only a small detachment that was responsible for Pilate's security in Herod's palace. But the more important issue is not where it took place but the Scriptural background it would have suggested to the evangelist and to those who read his words.

The Gentile reader would perhaps recall the standard acclamation of the emperor – Ave Caesar Imperator. Jewish readers might have seen in the mockery a repetition of the mockery of the prophets – for example of Jeremiah: 'I am ridiculed all day long, everyone mocks me . . . the word of the Lord has brought me insult and reproach all day long' (Jer. 20:7,8). Both Jews and Gentiles remembered that Jesus actually predicted, or so it seemed, this precise circumstance: 'They will condemn him [the son of man] to death and will turn him over to the Gentiles, who will mock him and spit on him, flog him and kill him' (Mark 10:33–4). One of the striking features of this narrative is the constant claim that what was happening here in Jerusalem on this Friday morning had been predicted, and could be regarded as the fulfilment of God's intention for the world.

The Encounter

It is at this point that Simon of Cyrene comes on the scene. He was passing by on his way in 'from the country', which probably meant not that he was travelling in from his own farm as a Cyrenian resident in Palestine, but that he was there on pilgrimage, intending nothing more than to fulfil his religious duties and then go back home again to Africa. It was, he must have thought, an odd circumstance that he, a visitor in Jerusalem, should be seized on by the Roman detachment, as was their right, to carry the cross of a condemned revolutionary leader. He had no doubt seen crucifixions before in his own troubled province, but this was the first time he had ever been involved in one. It was an unhappy omen for his day of celebration, a painful experience to have to relate to his relatives back at home.

And who was this man anyway for whom he was carrying the cross, and what could he have done to deserve this most cruel of all Roman punishments – this blood-bespattered, exhausted figure making his way down his own Via Dolorosa? This was indeed an odd encounter; and in the course of it something must have happened in his mind which changed the direction of his life.

The fact that Mark alone records the names of his sons is significant. He would not have bothered with this detail, even if he had been aware of it, if the names were not in some sense likely to be significant to his readers. Both names occur elsewhere in the New Testament, but as the names were common, no exact identification is possible. However, they would not have been mentioned if Mark had not expected to elicit from the congregation some recognition that they were members of the Church, either in Rome or in Cyrene itself.

At some point in that horrific, unforgettable day, the seed of new life was sown in the hearts of Simon and his family. It is interesting that John, in his gospel, does not mention the part played by Simon of Cyrene and, indeed, seems to exclude it by his phrase in John 19:17: 'Carrying his own cross, he [Jesus] went out to the place of the Skull'. In the author's mind, this may have been to guard against a theory propounded in his day that at the last moment Simon of Cyrene had been substituted for Jesus and that Jesus had never died.

Such theories have surfaced from time to time ever since, but it seems to the present author that if there is one event of which we can be absolutely sure in the history of the world it is that Jesus was tried by the Roman governor, was crucified and died later that Friday afternoon.

The Crucifixion

The site of the crucifixion cannot be identified with any certainty. What is reasonably certain is that, in accordance with the normal Roman procedure, the condemned men would have been executed in a public place, preferably on the main road, to achieve maximum deterrence to any who might be contemplating subversive activity against the Roman state.

The drugged wine which Jesus refused may have been part of the provision by Jewish women for the assistance of 'patriots' who were suffering the extreme penalty. Mark does not say so. In fact, the narrative is remarkable for the many things that Mark does not say. There is no attempt to elicit sympathy for Jesus, no description of the horrors to which he and the two robbers were subjected, no mention of the midday sun beating down upon them, or of the agony of hanging there, suspended between heaven and earth for as long as the human body could endure it. The crucifixion is described in four words – 'and they crucified him'. Yet he does observe, mindful presumably of Psalm 22:16–18, that the execution party divided up his clothes, and cast lots to see what each would get: 'Dogs have surrounded me; a band of evil men have encircled me, they have pierced my hands and my feet. I can count all my bones; people stare and gloat over me, they divide my garments among them and cast lots for my clothing.'

The King of the Jews

The inscription which it was customary to attach to the accused or fix to the cross read 'the King of the Jews'. It was, in part, a last gesture by the procurator, enraged at being outwitted by the Jewish authorities, and in part a simple statement of fact – the man hanging there was the king of the Jews, the Messiah for whom Israel had fervently waited. So this was to be the end of the dream: the Messiah was crucified with two robbers – which merely served to enhance his guilt by association. To the last, the accusation was hurled in his face that he had predicted that he would destroy the Temple and build it in three days. Even the chief priests and the teachers of the Law mocked him – not publicly, it has to be said, but 'among themselves'.

The tribute of a man's enemies is sometimes the best tribute that can be paid to him. So for all their rage, his opponents acknowledged that he had saved others; the blind had had their sight restored; the deaf had had their ears opened; the lame had walked at his touch; lepers had been cleansed; and even the dead had been raised. There were countless men and women in Galilee who would rise up and call him blessed at the last day. These were indeed the 'signs of the Messiah', but the official leaders of Judaism were wholly oblivious to them. They would only believe if he came down from the cross.

Earlier in his life, the Pharisees had come and begun to question Jesus. They asked him for a sign from heaven. 'He sighed deeply and said, "Why does this generation ask for a miraculous sign? I tell you the truth, no sign will be given to it"' (Mark 8:11–12). There was no sign in heaven or on earth which would have convinced his opponents. They were irremediably lost. 'Is it nothing to you, all you who pass by?' (Lam. 1:12). No, it meant nothing to them – but that an imposter was receiving the due reward for his sins.

The Fulfilment of History

The story of the crucifixion is told, as is usual with Mark, with great restraint. The reader is not exposed as he would be by a modern documentary to the horrors of this agonising death. This is no doubt in part due to the fact that members of Mark's congregation would have been only too familiar with the sight of crucified men hanging by the wayside for their offences against the state. But it is also true that Mark had other more important things on his mind, and to these we now turn.

Behind the narrative is a whole series of biblical images from the Old Testament which would have been familiar to most of his readers. See, for example, Isaiah 50:5–9, Isaiah 53:4–9, the Wisdom of Solomon 2:10–20. The untutored reader studying this crucifixion passage could well read it without being aware of these images at all, but for Mark they comprised his understanding of the whole dread event which he had received in the tradition and was now transmitting to future generations. This does not mean, as has sometimes been asserted, that Mark is deliberately conforming his narrative to Old Testament patterns with which he was familiar; nor does it mean that he is slavishly depending on the so-called predictions of the Old Testament to account for what happened in Jerusalem that day.

Matthew, for example, does press some quotations from the Old Testament into the service of his story, but not so with Mark. He sees in the history of his people a certain 'drift' which leads inevitably to Calvary. In his view the Old Testament is a rehearsal of that history, showing over and over again how the man of God found himself opposed by the leaders of his own people:

> Woe to you, because you build tombs for the prophets, and it was your forefathers who killed them. So you testify that you approve of what your forefathers did; they killed the prophets, and you build their tombs. Because of this, God in his wisdom said, 'I will send them prophets and apostles, some of whom they will kill and others they will persecute.' Therefore this generation will be held responsible for the blood of all the prophets that has been shed since the beginning of the world, from the blood of Abel to the blood of Zechariah, who was killed between the altar and the sanctuary. Yes, I tell you, this generation will be held responsible for it all. (Luke 11:47–51)

So the trial and the crucifixion of Jesus was not a momentary aberration, or an action taken out of panic, but the natural outcome of a long historical process which began with the murder of Abel, was illustrated in the slaughter of Zechariah, and came to its final term in the execution of the Messiah. That accounts for a certain sense of inevitability which emerges from the narrative. '. . . it cannot be,' Jesus had said, 'that a prophet should perish away from Jerusalem' (Luke 13:33 RSV).

The World Stage

The second element in Mark's understanding of his narrative arises out of the circumstances under which Jesus was tried and executed. If he had been convicted in a Jewish court, and if that court had had the power to execute the sentence of death, Jesus would have been stoned. But in the end he was not convicted of an offence against religion, but of treason against the state. It was therefore in a Roman court that he was judged and a Roman punishment to which he was sentenced. It was an event which was to have reverberations throughout the empire.

So Mark is insisting this was not just a storm in a Jewish teacup but an event on a world stage. Jesus was tried and executed not simply as a consequence of a squalid plot in a distant provincial city; he was tried and executed before a tribunal which represented no less than the emperor himself in Rome. If I may put it thus, what happened on that Friday morning was not simply an item for the local newspaper, but for the world press.

The World Mission

The third element in Mark's understanding of the Passion arises from the fact that he was the companion of Paul and Barnabas in the earliest missionary enterprises of the Church. He would remember that Paul himself had acted for the Jewish authorities in Jerusalem, seeking to extinguish the growing Christian movement in Damascus (Acts 9). Subsequently Paul found himself in the other camp and consequently at risk from those same authorities in Judea who sought to overturn his work in the synagogues of the Dispersion.

At Antioch, for example, 'men came down from Judea . . . and were teaching the brothers: "Unless you are circumcised according to the custom taught by Moses, you cannot be saved"' (Acts 15:1).

Paul's preaching had created dissension not simply between Christians and Jews but between Christians of one school and Christians of another, and the council of Jerusalem recorded in Acts 15 was an early attempt, not wholly successful, to arrive at a concordat between the Christians of

the diaspora who wished to be free of the burden of the Jewish
Law, and the Christians of Judea who saw the Law in all its
rigor as still binding upon the new Christian community. It is
perhaps not surprising that in the end Paul himself paid the
penalty for his own 'liberal' views when he was arrested in
Jerusalem, tried by the Sanhedrin, and ultimately committed
to the authorities in Rome.

It is no accident that Paul, like Jesus before him, went 'to
Jerusalem, bound in the Spirit, not knowing what shall befall
me there' (Acts 20:22 RSV). It is against this background of
the early decades of Christian history that the sudden appearance of Simon of Cyrene in the Passion narrative is best
understood. It was a member of the Dispersion who was the
first to carry the cross of Christ. He and his family were not
just people: they were representatives of a movement nur-
tured in the heart of Judaism which was ultimately to become
a threat to Judaism.

The Sons of Abraham

The fourth element in Mark's understanding of the Passion
derives from his attitude to the rulers of his people, created
not only by their treatment of Jesus, but their unfailing
opposition to Jesus's followers in Judea and in the diaspora.
It is not on that account to be presumed that he misrep-
resented their actions in the trial and crucifixion of Jesus,
because in the end those actions speak for themselves. Even
Pilate saw that it was 'from envy that they had delivered Jesus
to him'. But it has to be observed that Mark consistently
makes a clear distinction between the Jewish people as a
whole and their rulers at that particular juncture in their
history.

Jesus himself had made that same distinction when he said
to the crowd and to his disciples: 'The teachers of the law and
the Pharisees sit in Moses' seat. So you must obey them and
do everything they tell you. But do not do what they do, for
they do not practise what they preach' (Matt. 23:1–3). Simon
of Cyrene was not a Jew of Jerusalem, but he was a Jew

nevertheless, of the seed of Abraham, a loyal Jew, who came all the way from the North African coast to be present at the Passover. It was a Jew who carried Christ's cross. It was Jews who followed Jesus in his earthly ministry; and it was Jews who proclaimed the truth of Jesus in the ancient world. It was Jews who were leaders of the Church – and Jesus was a Jew.

If Mark had not learned the lesson anywhere else, he would certainly have learned this lesson from Paul, who never made any secret of his abiding love for his own people despite all that he had suffered at their hands (Rom. 11:25–32). Salvation is of the Jews. 'Theirs is the adoption as sons; theirs the divine glory, the covenants, the receiving of the law, the temple worship and the promises. Theirs are the patriarchs, and from them is traced the human ancestry of Christ, who is God over all, for ever praised' (Rom. 9:4–5). Paul ends that particular passage with the word 'Amen'. For all the hideous injustice perpetrated by their leaders on that Friday morning, we still must echo that joyful 'Amen' when we consider that it was a Jew who suffered these, not only for his own people but for every nation under heaven:

> Oh, the depth of the riches of the wisdom and
> knowledge of God!
> How unsearchable his judgments, and his
> paths beyond tracing out!
> Who has known the mind of the Lord?
> Or who has been his counsellor?
> Who has ever given to God,
> that God should repay him?
> For from him and through him and to him
> are all things.
> To him be the glory for ever! Amen. (Rom. 11:33–6)

19

THE CENTURION

[Mark 15:33–41]

[33]At the sixth hour darkness came over the whole land until the ninth hour. [34]And at the ninth hour Jesus cried out in a loud voice, *"Eloi, Eloi, lama sabachthani?"*—which means, "My God, my God, why have you forsaken me?"

[35]When some of those standing near heard this, they said, "Listen, he's calling Elijah."

[36]One man ran, filled a sponge with wine vinegar, put it on a stick, and offered it to Jesus to drink. "Now leave him alone. Let's see if Elijah comes to take him down," he said.

[37]With a loud cry, Jesus breathed his last.

[38]The curtain of the temple was torn in two from top to bottom.

[39]And when the centurion, who stood there in front of Jesus, heard his cry and saw how he died, he said, "Surely this man was the Son of God!"

[40]Some women were watching from a distance. Among them were Mary Magdalene, Mary the mother of James the younger and of Joses, and Salome. [41]In Galilee these women had followed him and cared for his needs. Many other women who had come up with him to Jerusalem were also there.

With this passage we move into the 'heart of darkness', a darkness which has in the end proved to be luminous with truth and joy for a large section of the human race ever since. We tread on holy ground, and an 'expressive silence' as Richard Glover puts it in his commentary (Marshall, Morgan and Scott, 1957) is the only proper approach to it. But the silence may come to be more expressive still when certain aspects of this drama are more clearly understood.

Nevertheless, in dealing with what may seem to be trifling details in the story, I am conscious of treading where angels fear to tread and where even the greatest theologians falter.

This encounter with the centurion is the third of the trio of encounters which take place within a single day and within a single locality – Pilate, representing the majesty of Roman law, Simon representing worldwide Judaism far beyond the bounds of Judea itself, and now the centurion, representing the might of an oppressive empire now involved in an unwelcome and disagreeable duty, thinking perhaps thoughts of home and family, cursing his luck out there in the midday sun, eager to have the business over and get back to tea, but watchful, nevertheless, as he would need to be in the presence of a volatile crowd in a dangerous country, in a world violently hostile to Roman arms.

The Army

The centurion, variously named in tradition as Longinus or Petronius, would have been the equivalent of a company commander in the modern British army, commanding – as the title suggests – one hundred men. He could have been recruited anywhere within the boundaries of the Roman empire. He could even have been a Jew or a Samaritan: both had a warlike reputation and were welcomed into the Roman army. But it is more likely, in view of the local political situation, that he would have been recruited in Egypt or Greece or Syria, and was now on 'an overseas posting'.

The unit of the Roman army with which we are most familiar is the legion, comprising 5,000 men. The legion would have been divided into five cohorts, or bands, commanded by a tribune. Each cohort therefore would have ten centurions. Centurions had little chance of promotion beyond that rank and they were treated as figures of fun by the sophisticated writers of antiquity for their crudity and lack of education. But they were the backbone of the army, associated in the closest possible way with the troops under their command, and, in the eyes of the public, the typical representatives of Roman power and ruthlessness.

For most of the empire's life there was no shortage of recruits. They could see the world, they could be assured of some plunder, they could look forward to an adequate pension and a family house in one of the military-style settlements on the imperial frontiers. But it was a tough and dangerous life; no one would expect a centurion to be unduly sensitive to other people's feelings or introspective about his own. They were men of action, trained to obey without hesitation.

So here he was, this Longinus or Petronius, in charge of an execution party, doing what he had done many times before, and would no doubt do many times again – exercising vengeance upon those who had the temerity to confront the might of Rome. His not to reason why, his just to do and help others to die. Before we look in detail at the events in which he was involved on this Friday morning, we must try to clarify in our minds what St Mark actually wrote, as distinct from the extra material we find in the other three evangelists.

Matthew, Luke and John

Matthew, as usual, follows his source carefully, but he does add extra elements to it which come from his particular tradition. He tends here, as elsewhere, to emphasise the supernatural and visual phenomena. It is to him that we owe the story of the earthquake and the resurrection of many of God's people who came out of their tombs and after Jesus's resurrection went into the holy city and appeared to many people.

Luke adds Jesus's prayer for his opponents – 'Father forgive them, for they do not know what they are doing' (Luke 23:34). He tells the story of the penitent thief and of Jesus's response to him. 'I tell you the truth, today you will be with me in paradise' (Luke 23:43). And Luke adds to the 'loud cry' which Mark also records, the prayer, 'Father, into your hands I commit my spirit' (Luke 23:46).

John's treatment of the narrative is different and seems, a

times, to be at variance with Mark. He alone among the evangelists records that the mother of Jesus was present at the crucifixion and that Jesus committed her into the hands of the beloved disciple – '"Dear woman, here is your son," and to the disciple, "Here is your mother"' (John 19:26). Mark records that Jesus was given a drink; in John's account this is preceded by Jesus's cry, 'I am thirsty' (John 19:28), and the long ordeal ends with the triumphant cry from the cross, 'It is finished' (John 19:30). Subsequently the soldiers, according to John, came and broke the legs of the two robbers, but when they found that Jesus was already dead they did not break his legs. One of the soldiers pierced Jesus's side with a spear, causing a sudden flow of blood and water (John 19:32–4).

As I dictate these words I realise for myself how much I have harboured in my own mind of this extra material from Matthew, Luke and John. To turn back to the Marcan narrative is to realise how brief and unembellished his story of the crucifixion is – a mere seven verses for the event which was to change the direction of history for ever. I do not propose to discuss the many technical issues which arise on this passage, but rather to concentrate on those elements in it which in Mark's mind were essential for the understanding of what it was that happened on Friday morning between nine o'clock and three o'clock in the afternoon. There would have been three elements in this story which would have been of the greatest interest to Mark's readers in Rome and elsewhere in the Jewish diaspora. They are the cry of dereliction and the reference to Elijah, the rending of the curtain of the Temple, and the centurion's affirmation of faith.

The Cry of Dereliction

It is not surprising that Luke and John did not record the cry of dereliction. Even if they were aware of it they might well have hesitated to record something which could suggest that Jesus had lost faith in his Father, or even that he had been mistaken all along. Indeed so strange did it seem to later readers of the gospel that one scribe substituted for 'Why have you forsaken me?' the phrase 'Why have you given me over to reproach?' But the text we have in front of us is undoubtedly the right one. We must account for it as it stands. The words are from Psalm 22:

> My God, my God, why have you forsaken me?
> Why are you so far from saving me, so far
> from the words of my groaning?
> O my God, I cry out by day, but you do not
> answer, by night, and am not silent. (Ps. 22:1–2)

The psalm as a whole is the cry of a just man who in the midst of his troubles feels that he has been forsaken by God, but who by the end of the psalm is full of assurance about God's love and care for him:

> All the ends of the earth will remember and
> turn to the Lord, and all the families of the
> nations will bow down before him, for dominion
> belongs to the Lord and he rules over the nations.
> (Ps. 22:27–8)

The psalm was of great importance in the life of the early Church not just because of its use here, but because it typified not only the sufferings of the Messiah but the sufferings of all God's people under persecution from the rich and the powerful. But these words of Jesus from the cross were misunderstood not only by later members of the early Church, but by some of the bystanders on the day itself. The word for God (Eloi) suggested to some that he was calling for Elijah. That would not have been surprising to a Jew because Elijah had long enjoyed the reputation of coming to the aid of loyal Jews in their time of need. To Mark this would have been an instructive mistake because according to tradition it was Elijah who was to herald the coming of the Messiah and it was Elijah who had actually appeared to Jesus at the Transfiguration.

The rending of the curtain

The 'curtain of the Temple' is normally understood to be the curtain which hung between the holy place and the holy of holies through which, once a year only, the High Priest, and he alone, passed for the atonement of the people. It marked off the Temple in general from the innermost shrine of God's presence. Only the High Priest enjoyed the supreme privilege of speaking to God face to face, and for that privilege he was meticulously prepared in an elaborate ritual. The theological significance of this incident has been spelled out for us by the writer of the Epistle to the Hebrews:

> Since we have confidence to enter the Most Holy Place by the blood of Jesus, by a new and living way opened for us through the curtain, that is, his body, and since we have a great priest over the house of God, let us draw near to God with a sincere heart in full assurance of faith, having our hearts sprinkled to cleanse us from a guilty conscience and having our bodies washed with pure water. (Heb. 10:19–22)

So, the author is saying, the rending of the body of Jesus was at the same time a rending of the curtain which had stood between the believer and an experience of the living God. The Temple system, for all its rich associations with the past and its incalculable effects on the history of Israel, was to be done away. The witnesses at the trial had given evidence of some such prophecy by Jesus. Now it had come to pass. The Jews remained, for good or ill, a chosen people, but their exclusive privileges had been withdrawn for ever. The Law of God given to Moses at Sinai was now a law for all. The access to the divine presence limited to the few, was accessible to everyone. The Temple had become for a short time pending its final destruction 'a House of Prayer for all nations'.

There could hardly be a more important message for Mark's congregation than that, troubled as they were by the growing rift between Jewish and Gentile members of the congregation, and by mounting opposition from the Jerusalem establishment. But we cannot shirk the question: Did it really happen? Legends abound. Josephus records strange

events which happened forty years before the destruction of
the Temple in AD 70 (i.e. at about the time of the crucifixion) –
a great light was seen, and the eastern gate opened of its own
accord. In the gospel according to the Hebrews the lintel of
the Temple fell down in fragments.

But there is a difference between the portents thus described and Mark's account – the rending of the Temple
curtain is not regarded by him as a great public display
intended to convince or to alarm. It was a hidden sign, later to
be disclosed, of the coming judgment upon the Temple and
the priesthood which served it. Mark was not the first or the
last to be aware of a curious correspondence occasionally to
be observed between 'spiritual events' and physical events;
the secret rending of the Temple curtain coincided with the
only too public event at Calvary. Both were signs of the
coming judgment: '. . . do not weep for me, but . . . for your
children' (Luke 23:28). We have no means of knowing the
source of Mark's information, but I am inclined to take his
account at its face value – 'the curtain of the temple was torn
in two from top to bottom'.

The centurion's confession of faith

Centurions on the whole get a good press in the New Testament. In a passage in Matthew's gospel, unrecorded in Mark,
a centurion comes to Jesus begging help for his servant who is
desperately ill, but insists that Jesus should not bother to
come to his house because, he said,

> For I myself am a man under authority, with soldiers under me. I
> tell this one, 'Go,' and he goes; and that one, 'Come,' and he
> comes. I say to my servant, 'Do this,' and he does it . . . Jesus was
> astonished and said to those following him, 'I tell you the truth, I
> have not found anyone in Israel with such great faith. I say to you
> that many will come from the east and the west, and will take
> their places at the feast with Abraham, Isaac and Jacob in the
> kingdom of heaven. But the subjects of the kingdom will be
> thrown outside, into the darkness, where there will be weeping
> and gnashing of teeth.' (Matthew 8:9–12)

In Acts 10:22, Cornelius, the centurion who had sent for Peter, is described as a 'righteous and God-fearing man who is respected by all the Jewish people'. Paul was saved from a flogging on the initiative of the centurion who took it upon himself to report to his commander that Paul was a Roman citizen (Acts 22:23–8). It was a centurion who saved Paul from almost certain death when the ship in which he was travelling to Rome was shipwrecked (Acts 27:42–4).

It can be argued that Christian writers would have been eager to exhibit the Roman state and the Roman army in the best possible light in order to dispel any suspicion that the Christian Church was a treasonable body, but Matthew has no such object in mind when he records Jesus's astonishment at the faith of the centurion in Capernaum. Mark in his account of the crucifixion is at pains only to emphasise the extraordinary fact that it was a Roman soldier who was the first to make the affirmation that subsequently became part of the early creed of the Church. He offers no psychological reason for it, perhaps for the simple reason that he did not know one.

The centurion was a hardened soldier who was used to executions of this kind, and was unlikely to have been unduly disturbed by feelings of pity or compassion for those he ushered so painfully into the next world. But it is possible that Mark wishes us to understand that he had treated Jesus with some humanity; he had found someone to carry his cross; he had at least permitted drink to be offered to the suffering man.

So there may have been something in the events of that day which prepared the centurion for his remarkable utterance. He would undoubtedly have accompanied the governor at the trial, and may have been impressed, as obviously Pilate was, by the majestic silence with which Jesus confronted his accusers. He may have been convinced, as Pilate was, that the prisoner was being wrongly accused.

Matthew suggests that it was the supernatural events of that afternoon which so impressed the centurion – the earthquake, the darkness, the opening of the tombs (Matt. 27:51–3). But in Mark no such suggestion is made; he records baldly that it was 'when he heard Jesus cry and saw how he died' that he responded in awe with the words 'Surely this man was the Son of God.' Mark, of course, is not suggesting that the centurion had received a revelation about the inner nature of Jesus, which was later to be the subject of learned debate for many centuries in the Church.

Luke, no doubt puzzled by the centurion's reaction, offers instead: 'The centurion, seeing what had happened, praised God and said, "Surely this was a righteous man"' (Luke 23:47). But this was not what Mark intended. The dispute as to whether the phrase should read 'a son of God' or 'the son of God' calls for too fine a distinction. The phrase 'Son of God' would have taken Mark right back to the beginning of the story, when Jesus heard a voice at his baptism saying 'You are my Son whom I love; with you I am well pleased' (Mark 1:11). We are in no position to judge exactly what the centurion meant or how he felt. He was a soldier, untrained in metaphysics. He probably felt what Napoleon many centuries later is reported to have said: 'I know men. And I can tell you that this man [Jesus] is no ordinary man.' In his view, there was something supernatural in the way this young Jewish man died.

But from Mark's point of view it was a confession of faith. This rough soldier, despised by the rulers of Israel no doubt as a heathen man without any spiritual sensitivities whatsoever sees through the pain, the darkness, the blood and the cries of the bereaved, a glimpse of the divine, which for all their learning and zeal the rulers of Israel had failed to see. The 'suffering servant' had won his first victory from the cross. The Roman centurion at Calvary joined hands with the Roman centurion in Capernaum to confess him as the Messiah.

The disclosure is now complete, affirmed by a series of witnesses, of whom the centurion is the last. The Messianic secret is out, and the world awaits God's public vindication of his beloved son. God had not forsaken him.

20

THE LAST ENCOUNTER

[Mark 15:42–16:8]

^{42}It was Preparation Day (that is, the day before the Sabbath). So as evening approached, ^{43}Joseph of Arimathea, a prominent member of the Council, who was himself waiting for the kingdom of God, went boldly to Pilate and asked for Jesus' body. ^{44}Pilate was surprised to hear that he was already dead. Summoning the centurion, he asked him if Jesus had already died. ^{45}When he learned from the centurion that it was so, he gave the body to Joseph. ^{46}So Joseph bought some linen cloth, took down the body, wrapped it in the linen, and placed it in a tomb cut out of rock. Then he rolled a stone against the entrance of the tomb. ^{47}Mary Magdalene and Mary the mother of Joses saw where he was laid.

16 When the Sabbath was over, Mary Magdalene, Mary the mother of James, and Salome bought spices so that they might go to anoint Jesus' body. ^{2}Very early on the first day of the week, just after sunrise, they were on their way to the tomb ^{3}and they asked each other, "Who will roll the stone away from the entrance of the tomb?"

^{4}But when they looked up, they saw that the stone, which was very large, had been rolled away. ^{5}As they entered the tomb, they saw a young man dressed in a white robe sitting on the right side, and they were alarmed.

^{6}"Don't be alarmed," he said. "You are looking for Jesus the Nazarene, who was crucified. He has risen! He is not here. See the place where they had laid him. ^{7}But go, tell his disciples and Peter, 'He is going ahead of you into Galilee. There you will see him, just as he told you.'"

^{8}Trembling and bewildered, the women went out and fled from the tomb. They said nothing to anyone, because they were afraid.

Strictly speaking there is no encounter with the living Christ
recorded in this passage. It has to be regarded rather as the
prelude to a series of encounters recorded in the other gospels
and, by inference, the encounter with the living Christ which
confronts every reader of the gospel. But this calls for some
elucidation of the problem which is normally handled under
this heading:

The Lost Ending of Mark

Almost all modern translations of the gospel end at Mark
16:8: 'They said nothing to anyone, because they were afraid.'
What follows in earlier translations of the gospel is, in the
almost unanimous verdict of the scholars, not part of the
original gospel at all. One can seldom speak of 'an unanimous
verdict' in the field of New Testament scholarship, but this is
one of the few examples. Even in the English translation
verses 9–20 seem to be at variance with the style and the
language of the rest of the gospel, and in the original Greek it
is even more evident.

But the most telling argument of all is that whereas in the
first sixteen and a half chapters Mark is relying on his own
sources of information, in this latter half of the sixteenth
chapter the author is drawing on sources which would not
have been available at the end of the sixties when Mark wrote.
For example, he seems to rely on passages in Luke and John
which come from the latter part of the first century. In
addition, Matthew – who otherwise follows the Marcan narrative fairly closely – here departs from it entirely and provides
an ending (chapter 28) which is quite distinct. But if it is not
part of the original gospel this leaves us with a problem – the
problem of 'the lost ending'.

There are scholars, whom I greatly admire, who say that
there is no 'lost ending' because the author intended the
gospel to end at verse 8. There are weighty arguments in
favour of that assertion – not least that there is absolutely no
trace anywhere in the documentary history of an ending
which can be safely attributed to Mark. On the other side it

has to be said that it is almost unthinkable that any writer would have chosen to end his book with the words 'because they were afraid'. In the Greek it would have been even more extraordinary because he would have made his gospel end with the word 'for'. So, rather reluctantly, I have had to conclude that the ending has in fact been lost – and lost for ever.

In the principate of Nero it would not have been impossible that a knock at the door during the night could have ended Mark's freedom and even his life. It is not impossible that the last page of the manuscript was lost before the book saw the light of day in a Roman congregation, and certainly long before it became part of the Bible of the early Church.

The importance of this issue for us who are seeking primarily to understand Mark's view of the Passion and resurrection of Christ is that we cannot rely on Mark for any 'resurrection appearances'. We may infer or we may speculate or we may have opinions, but the fact is that we cannot cite Mark as evidence for them. But we can cite Mark for one all-important feature of the record of those few days in Jerusalem – and it is that the tomb was empty. 'He has risen. He is not here. See the place where they laid him.' Jesus had died on Friday afternoon, he had been buried on Friday evening: now the tomb was empty.

The Burial

Executed criminals would normally have been buried in a common grave and within a few months no one would remember where they had been buried. They just ceased to be – without any record of their doings, with no headstone and no epitaph, no flowers. The body of Jesus was saved from this fate by the courageous act of a man named Joseph who came, it is said, from Arimathea, a village which cannot with certainty be identified, but could have been a village some five miles north of Jerusalem.

He is variously described in the gospels, for example: 'Joseph, who had himself become a disciple of Jesus' (Matt.

27:57); 'a man named Joseph, a member of the Council, a good and upright man, who had not consented to their decision and action' (Luke 23:51); 'Joseph was a disciple of Jesus, but secretly because he feared the Jews' (John 19:38). Mark describes him as a 'prominent member of the Council who was himself waiting for the kingdom of God'.

It seems likely therefore that Joseph was, though it is not undisputed, a member of the Sanhedrin and one of the few who opposed Jesus's arrest and conviction. According to Mark he went 'boldly' to Pilate and asked for the body – 'boldly', because he was by then no doubt suspect to his own peers in the Sanhedrin as a secret disciple of the man they believed to be an imposter, and because it would take a bold man to risk a confrontation with the procurator at the end of a busy and frustrating day. According to the apocryphal 'Gospel of Peter' Joseph was 'a friend of Pilate'. This may have been intended as an explanation of why Pilate responded so favourably to the unusual request.

Mark and Matthew do not say where the tomb was. Luke says that it was 'a tomb cut in the rock, one in which no-one had yet been laid' (Luke 23:53). John is slightly more explicit when he says that: 'At the place where Jesus was crucified, there was a garden, and in the garden a new tomb, in which no-one had ever been laid. Because it was the Jewish day of Preparation and since the tomb was near by, they laid Jesus there' (John 19:41–2). The tradition that it was the tomb cut out of the rock by Joseph for himself and for his family gains some support from Matthew 27:60, and from the fact that there was a garden in Jerusalem known to antiquity as 'Joseph's garden'. But the exact location cannot now be determined despite a thriving tourist traffic to the Church of the Holy Sepulchre and to an alternative site known as 'the Garden Tomb' outside the present city wall.

After centuries of war and devastation, of building and rebuilding, certainty is no longer available to us, but the location of the tomb was certainly known to Jesus's disciples and probably to the Jewish authorities as well.

'Mary Magdalene and Mary the mother of Jesus saw where he was laid' (Mark 15:47); 'Mary Magdalene and the other

Mary were sitting there opposite the tomb' (Matt. 27:61);
'The women who had come with Jesus from Galilee followed
Joseph and saw the tomb and how his body was laid in it'
(Luke 23:55). All the evangelists mention the stone which was
rolled in front of the entrance to the tomb. But Matthew goes
further than the others. He records that:

> The next day, the one after Preparation Day, the chief priests and
> the Pharisees went to Pilate. 'Sir,' they said, 'we remember that
> while he was still alive that deceiver said, "After three days I will
> rise again." So give the order for the tomb to be made secure until
> the third day. Otherwise, his disciples may come and steal the
> body and tell the people that he has been raised from the dead.
> This last deception will be worse than the first.' 'Take a guard,'
> Pilate answered. 'Go, make the tomb as secure as you know
> how.' So they went and made the tomb secure by putting a seal on
> the stone and posting the guard. (Matthew 27:62–6)

There is nothing inherently improbable in this additional
narrative. 'The three days' figures prominently in the gospels
and the chief priests could well have been afraid of some such
stratagem as they reported to Pilate. Pilate himself would see
no reason for refusing the request and certainly was not
disposed to risk further trouble in what had proved to be a
highly embarrassing incident.

It seems unlikely, however, that he would have provided a
detachment of soldiers from among his own troops. After all,
a member of the Sanhedrin had now taken charge of the body
and had buried it in his own garden. It would be up to the
Jewish authorities to provide a detachment from among their
own temple guard to keep watch in the garden. Thus the
location of the tomb would have been known to a number of
people in addition to the disciples. Yet the following morning,
despite the stone and the seal and the guard, the tomb was
empty.

The empty tomb

It is not surprising that a huge body of literature has grown up around this issue. It continues to affront human reason and to defy human imagination. The gospel narratives themselves differ from each other, sometimes quite substantially, about the order of events on that Sunday morning (see Matthew 28, Luke 24, John 20). In John it was Mary Magdalene alone who arrived first. In Matthew it is 'Mary Magdalene and the other Mary'. In Luke it is the 'women who took the spices they had prepared'. And in Mark it is 'Mary Magdalene, Mary the mother of Jesus, and Salome'. Matthew, Luke and John agree that the first witnesses ran to tell the other disciples. Mark says that 'they said nothing to anyone because they were afraid'. But all the evangelists agree that the tomb was empty – a testimony made all the more impressive by the variation in other matters of detail.

What then are we, members of a sceptical, sophisticated society, to say about this seemingly inexplicable event? Of one thing we can be sure – everything we can say has been said before. The chief priests and the elders gave the soldiers of the guard a large sum of money telling them to say that his disciples came during the night and stole him away while they were asleep (Matt. 28:12–14).

It was a desperate throw, and even members of the Sanhedrin, knowing what they did about the disciples, would find it difficult to believe. How could the handful of dispirited men have evaded the guard, moved the stone, taken away the body, without waking anyone up? The only other people who knew in which tomb Jesus had been buried would have been members of the Sanhedrin, the procurator, and Joseph of Arimathea himself. There seems no reason to suppose that any of these would have profited from presenting to the world the following morning an empty tomb.

There are realistically only three other possibilities. The first is that the women had made a mistake about the locality of the tomb. But they had seen him buried there on Friday night. If it was in Joseph's garden there would have been only one tomb, in which ultimately he and his family would expect to be buried. Cutting into rock was an arduous and expensive business. Provision would have been made for ample space inside the tomb. It would therefore have been a substantial feature, not easy to miss.

The second is that Jesus was not really dead at all and recovered in the tomb. This is a variation on the theory that it was Simon of Cyrene who was crucified, not Jesus himself. To the best of my knowledge there is not a single record in antiquity of a crucified man, certified dead by the centurion in charge, ever recovering from the ordeal.

The third possibility is the one supported by all the evangelists. It is that the tomb was empty and that the occupant of it subsequently appeared to his disciples in some 'bodily' form:

> Brothers, I can tell you confidently that the patriarch David died and was buried, and his tomb is here to this day. But he was a prophet and knew that God had promised him on oath that he would place one of his descendants on his throne. Seeing what was ahead, he spoke of the resurrection of the Christ, that he was not abandoned to the grave, nor did his body see decay. God had raised this Jesus to life, and we are all witnesses of the fact. (Acts 2:29–32)

'We are all witnesses of the fact.' This is a confident utterance on behalf of Peter and the other disciples, and it was based initially on the undeviating testimony that the tomb was empty. We turn therefore now to:

The Resurrection Appearances

The earliest written account of the resurrection appearances is to be found not in the gospels but in Paul's first letter to the Corinthians written about AD 53, that is to say some years before Mark's gospel in its present form saw the light of day: this account is of particular importance because it comes from one who was not part of the apostolic band and had not been involved in any way in the events surrounding the crucifixion. He had no 'gospels' as such to refer to. His account is about

what he 'received' from the earliest traditions of the Church.
Here it is in full:

> For what I received I passed on to you as of first importance: that
> Christ died for our sins according to the Scriptures, that he was
> buried, that he was raised on the third day according to the
> Scriptures, and that he appeared to Peter, and then to the
> Twelve. After that, he appeared to more than five hundred of
> the brothers at the same time, most of whom are still living,
> though some have fallen asleep. Then he appeared to James, then
> to all the apostles, and last of all he appeared to me also, as to
> one abnormally born. For I am the least of the apostles and do
> not even deserve to be called an apostle, because I persecuted
> the church of God. (1 Cor. 15:3–9)

His account is mirrored, in part, by the gospels, which
likewise refer to an appearance to Peter (Luke 24:34; John
21:15) and to the eleven (Luke 24:36; Matthew 28:16; John
20:24). He records an appearance to James, the brother of
Jesus, which does not appear in the canonical gospels,
although it is in the apocryphal gospel according to the
Hebrews. He refers also to an appearance to five hundred
brethren at once – an appearance which finds no place in the
gospels.

Those who are sensitive to such things will observe that
Paul does not refer to 'the women' at all. But this has to be
seen in the light of Paul's purpose in writing this letter to the
Corinthians. His authority in the church was always at risk
because he had not been a member of the Twelve, and as far as
is known never met Jesus in the flesh. So he is particularly
concerned in this letter to establish his credentials as an
apostle and to appeal to a common tradition which all the
apostles shared. He is not out to establish the truth of the
resurrection; in his mind there was no doubt about it. His
argument is based upon the assumption that the tomb was
empty and that Jesus had risen from the dead – and indeed his
experience on the Damascus road and his whole subsequent
ministry would have been unintelligible except on this
assumption.

But for all the importance of this independent testimony

by the last of the apostles, it still leaves us with a major difficulty in reconciling the gospel accounts of the resurrection appearances. The confusions of that fateful Easter morning have left their mark on the gospel records. There are (including the Pauline account) eleven identifiably separate appearances, but no amount of ingenuity has produced from them a generally agreed account of when and where they happened.

Matthew records a meeting with the women who had gone to the tomb (Matt. 28:8–10) and subsequently a meeting with the eleven disciples in Galilee (Matt. 28:16). Luke records an encounter with two disciples on the road to Emmaus (Luke 24:13–35) and subsequently to a meeting with the disciples in Jerusalem (including the report of an appearance to Peter). John records a meeting with Mary Magdalene (John 20:10–18, then, in the evening of that day, a meeting with the disciples, without Thomas, and a week later a meeting with the disciples and Thomas (John 20:24–30). Jesus subsequently meets his disciples by the Sea of Galilee and shares breakfast with them (John 21).

These variations need not concern us unduly. The writers of the gospels, with the possible exception of Mark, were not there when the resurrection happened. They are relying on the memories of those who were there, and who might be forgiven for not remembering in exact detail the course of that unprecedented experience. But the gospels agree that the tomb was empty and that it was the women (or a woman) who were first on the scene. The only point at which they seem positively to disagree is that according to Luke the disciples were commanded to stay in Jerusalem till Pentecost (Luke 24:49), but according to the other gospels they were commanded to go to Galilee where they would see Jesus again (Mark 16:7; Matt. 28:16; John 21:1). Many suggestions have been made to account for this discrepancy, but none of them is wholly convincing. It would be better to accept the fact that Luke, for theological rather than historical reasons, sees Jerusalem not only as the scene of Jesus's crucifixion and resurrection but as the centre of mission to the whole inhabited world (Luke 24:46–9). At this point we must turn back to Mark to consider the significance of the only authentic ending to the gospel which is known to us.

The Last Encounter

If there was an ending which through some mishap has been lost, it would have included appearances of the risen Christ to the disciples. 'There you will see him' (Mark 16:7). It is sometimes suggested that John 21 preserves this lost tradition – a point all the more relevant because John's narrative does include the so-called 'reinstatement' of Peter who is specifically referred to in Mark 16:7.

But Mark, as he laid down his pen at verse 8, may not have been thinking only or even primarily of the resurrection appearances which lay ahead. It was enough for him that the disciples would see Christ again. Failures, misunderstanding, the flight, the denial and even the betrayal, would be washed away in the transforming presence of the one whom, for all their inadequacies, they loved and adored. They would be back in Galilee, the past undone, back on the scene where they had first met Jesus of Nazareth and committed themselves to him, back on the scene of many wonderful works, of gracious teaching and rich companionship.

He had been dead (of that there was no doubt) 'and behold I am alive for ever and ever' (Rev. 1:18). But Mark looked beyond even that ravishing prospect, to the consummation of history, when he would come on the clouds and every eye would see him, even those who pierced him, and all the peoples of the earth would mourn because of him (Rev. 1:7). Then would be fulfilled the prophecy of Jesus on the Mount of Olives.

He had foretold that 'men will see the Son of Man coming in clouds with great power and glory. And he will send his angels and gather his elect from the four winds, from the ends of the earth to the ends of the heavens' (Mark 13:26–7). That would be the last great encounter, when the heavens roll back and the earth is stilled and Jesus is seated at the right hand of God.

There is another alternative ending to Mark in some manuscripts, and it goes like this:

> The women went to Peter and his friends and gave them a brief account of all that they had been told. After this Jesus himself sent out through his disciples from the east to the west the sacred and ever-living message of eternal salvation. (Mark 16:9–10)

This sacred and ever-living message of eternal salvation I, the author, commend to you, the reader.

REFLECTIONS

Uncertainty and Faith

This may be the first time some of my readers will have been introduced to the 'uncertainty factor' in the New Testament. There are variations within the same gospel between the oldest manuscripts available to us – most of them of little significance, but a few of them a source of controversy ever since. In such cases there is no way of achieving absolute certainty as to what the author originally wrote. Then there are variations between the gospels which cannot with any confidence be harmonised and there are uncertainties of interpretation arising from the fact that the authors wrote in a secular and religious environment which we do not share, and against a background we cannot wholly re-create.

The New Testament, like the Old Testament, did not drop down from heaven, ready made and bound in black. It has suffered the accidents of transmission which are common to all ancient literature, whether it be the classical Greek dramas, or Shakespeare. But the reader must not be alarmed – there are certain fixed points in a confusing scene on which a navigator may safely take his bearings.

First, the text we have in front of us is as good as painstaking textual scholarship can make it. We can rely on it as a faithful representation of what the authors in general intended, and it is unlikely that any future discoveries will seriously disturb the consensus that has been achieved. But second, we live not by certainty but by faith – faith in God, not in the authors, or the copyists or the scholars, in a God who spoke to the prophets through his Word and continues to speak to us. There may be flies on the window or flaws in the glass, but they do not seriously distort the view. The Bible has been exhaustively analysed down the centuries, and has stood the test as a convincing record of Israel's history up to the time of Jesus, and of the Christ-event itself as it was understood and proclaimed by the early Church.

Jews and Christians

As one who has been involved throughout my ministry in relationships between Jews and Christians I have been taken aback by the picture which emerges from the gospels of the persistent opposition Jesus encountered from his family and his nation. It is remorselessly chronicled by Mark from the very beginning of the ministry in Galilee to the climax of that opposition in Jerusalem. Even allowing for the fact that the evangelists will have been influenced by the conflict in their own day between the church and the synagogue, it makes for painful reading.

It is easy to see how the crude, uncritical use of the New Testament has led the way to the flagrant anti-Semitism which has disfigured the world ever since. There are, however, two saving observations which might be made. The first is that Mark is more careful than either Matthew or John to make a clear distinction between the people of Israel and their leaders. 'The great throng heard him gladly' (Mark 12:37 RSV), 'he had compassion on them, because they were like sheep without a shepherd' (Mark 6:34). In Jesus's view, the fault lay not with the lost sheep but with the false shepherds – a theme well developed by the prophet Ezekiel before him.

Second, Mark makes it abundantly clear that the proceedings against Jesus which led to his trial and crucifixion were initiated by the official leaders of Judaism – partly out of envy at his popularity among the ordinary people which had been generated by his ministry to them. Jesus's first followers were Jews, the leaders of the early Church were Jews, the New Testament was written by Jews (Luke was believed to be a proselyte). All that we know about Jesus we owe to the Jews. Jesus was a Jew. Rightly understood, the gospels provide no mandate for the savage treatment of the Jews by the Christian Church. To blame the Jews in general for the crucifixion is as reasonable as blaming a devout Spanish peasant of the fifteenth century for the gruesome excesses of the Inquisition.

Jesus, Man and God

The reactions to Jesus, as we have seen in Mark, were many and various. To his family he was just an embarrassing relative, to the rulers of Israel he was an imposter, to Herod Antipas, he was John the Baptist risen from the dead. To the generality of people he was a prophet or a teacher, 'powerful in word and deed' (Luke 24:19). To the disciples he was the Messiah. The centurion hailed him as 'son of God'. Peter, in his first recorded sermon, described him as 'Lord and Christ' (Acts 2:36). It was left to the doubting apostle, Thomas, to take the ultimate step of faith – 'My Lord and my God' (John 20:28).

This progression does not represent just an ascending scale of reverence in the early Church. It was of the essence of the Christ-event that it disclosed itself slowly, as minds were educated to receive it. When Jesus rose from the dead, he did more than move a stone and discard the containing graveclothes – he demolished the impressive intellectual edifices of the ancient world. No longer could men make the easy distinction between the human and the divine.

Paul was one of the first to perceive the nature of the revolution when he said – 'in Jesus, the complete being of God, by God's own choice, came to dwell' (Col. 1:19, NEB). This is a claim so staggering as to be beyond human comprehension – for ever. In moments of insight we may draw nearer the truth, then like a moth before a flame, we are dissolved by it. This for me has been one of the uncomfortable aspects of ministry – to have to speak for and to represent a shining truth which is for ever beyond my grasp, and mocks my attempts to articulate it for others. There are no easy answers. The Christ-event remains an unfathomable, though luminous mystery.

Jerusalem and Athens

Jerusalem was still intact when Mark's gospel was written, though even then under threat. The fall of the city in AD 70 was a cataclysmic event in the life of Israel. It spelt the end of the Temple and the priesthood and the loss of any central religious authority for worldwide Jewry. Such leadership as there was devolved upon a rabbinic centre of learning and jurisprudence in Jamnia on the coastal plain. It had an equally dramatic, though less obvious, effect on the future of the Christian Church. Some Christians escaped the carnage and fled to Pella in the Decapolis, some to Asia Minor, some to Alexandria or Greece. Jerusalem, therefore, and the Jewish Christian community there, ceased to be dominant or even influential in the life of the Church.

The centre of gravity had moved irrevocably west. Christian doctrine thus developed under the influence of Athens rather than of Jerusalem. The Old Testament was valued for the texts in it which foretold or prefigured the coming of Christ, but its understanding was no longer controlled by the Hebrew environment in which it had grown up. The leaders of the Church in the second and third centuries looked to Greek models for their understanding of the mystery of Christ. Our creeds are the product of that movement, and they are dominated by the sheer distinction, as the Greeks saw it, between the human and the divine.

In Hebrew theology, as represented by the Old Testament, the boundary between the human and the divine was infinitely flexible (see Judges 13 as an example). Mark would not have been unduly bothered by the philosophical problems which haunted the later Church as to how Jesus could have been both human and divine. Like his mentor Paul, he was a 'Hebrew of the Hebrews', and he would have learnt to be open to the transforming presence of God in nature, in history and in people. Many a bush burned with fire for such a man. His gospel therefore is free of any attempt to impose one dogmatic solution upon the mystery of Christ as it is re-presented in the encounters we have been studying. He would have been satisfied, if he had been aware of it, with

Matthew's allusion to Jesus as 'Emmanuel', which means 'God with us' (Matthew 1:23).

The People of the Way

Insofar as the first believers were differentiated from Judaism, they came to be known as 'Christians' (Acts 11:26) or as 'People of the Way' (Acts 9:2; 19:9, etc.). Mark's treatment of the Twelve, as we have seen, is unexpected. They are not written up as objects of veneration, and there is no suggestion that they are to be regarded as 'embryo' leaders of the Church. They were called to be evangelists ('fishers of men') and subsequently witnesses to the resurrection. In addition, they have a kind of exemplary role as the first of the 'people of the way' – who followed Jesus in the way from Capernaum to Caesarea, from Hermon to Jericho, from Bethany to Gethsemane. So the story of the Twelve was probably meant by Mark to be an encouragement and a warning to the would-be disciples of his own day, and remains relevant to Christian discipleship in our own day.

If a reader of this book finds himself drawn to Christ, he may be encouraged to know that, like the Twelve, he is not expected to understand everything before he begins 'in the way', and he need not be surprised at his failures, his disappointments, or even his seeming betrayals. Jesus having loved his own, loves them to the end (John 13:1). But there is warning, too, in the experience of the Twelve. He will have his moments of illumination and joy and peace, but the way does lead inevitably to some personal 'Calvary'. Jesus insisted that the Twelve must be prepared to take up the cross. Some of them literally did so: all of them paid a price for the privilege of following Jesus in the way. But in doing so he will discover for himself the truth of strength in weakness, victory out of defeat, glory even in shame. So may the Lord deny you peace and give you glory.

> I hear thee sung as mighty in the land
> I hear them hail thy bright ascendant star
> Hast thou no scar?
> . . .
> Can he have followed far who has no scar?
> (from Amy Carmichael, *Jerusalem*, SPCK).

The author and the book

Some authors put pen to paper only after they have achieved a clear perception of what their conclusions are to be, and of the stages by which they are to be reached. I am not among them. I have lavished many years on the detailed study of Mark's gospel, and I was reasonably sure of the 'encounters' I intended to describe. But after that, every chapter proved to be an adventure into disconcertingly unknown territory. Shades of meaning emerged of which I had not been previously aware; the story took on colours I had never perceived. I found myself at grips with a strong and subtle intelligence. I struggled to understand the Jewish and late-classical world in which Mark was reared and which he took for granted. I was drawn to unexpected conclusions; I was often surprised by the drift of Mark's thought. I shared the experience of most authors on the subject – the more I knew, the more I realised how little I knew. So this book is not a finished work, the climax of a long period of study. I have reached a staging-post, no more, and the conclusions I have reached and sought to communicate are of necessity interim and partial conclusions – until 'the day dawns, and the morning star rises in our hearts.'

Appendix A

SELECT BIBLIOGRAPHY

* Books which may be particularly helpful to the general reader

Commentaries

Anderson – Oliphants 1976
*Cranfield – Cambridge 1959
*Nineham – Pelican 1963
Rawlinson – Methuen 1925
Swete – Macmillan 1902
Taylor – Macmillan 1966

Books On Mark

Best – *Following Jesus* (Sheffield University, 1981)
*Best – *The Gospel as Story* (Clark, 1983)
Hengel – *Studies in the Gospel of Mark* (SCM, 1985)
*Hooker – *Message of Mark* (Epworth, 1983)
Lightfoot – *Gospel Message of Mark* (Oxford, 1950)
Martin – *Mark, Evangelist & Theologian* (Paternoster, 1972)
Marxsen – *Mark the Evangelist* (Abingdon, 1969)
Telford – *The Interpretation of Mark* (SPCK, 1985)
Trocmé – *Formation of the Gospel according to Mark* (SPCK, 1975)

Source Books

Brandon – *The Fall of Jerusalem and the Christian Church* (SCM, 1967)
*Harpers – *Bible Dictionary* (Harpers, 1985)
Hastings – *Dictionary of the Bible* (5 vols, 1898)

Hastings – *Dictionary of Christ and the Gospels* (2 vols, 1906)
Jeremias – *Jerusalem in the time of Jesus* (SCM, 1967)
Kittel – *Theological Dictionary of the New Testament* (10 vols, Eerdmans, 1964)
Metzger – *Textual Commentary on the Greek N.T.* (United Bible Societies, 1971)
*Rowland – *Christian Origins* (SPCK, 1985)
*G. A. Smith – *Historical Geography of the Holy Land* (Collins, 1973)
H. Smith – *Ante-Nicene Exegesis of the Gospels* (6 vols, SPCK, 1925)

Background Books

Ackroyd (ed.) – *Writings of the Jewish and Christian World* (8 vols, Cambridge, 1985)
Boardman (ed.) – *Oxford History of the Classical World* (1986)
*Bruce – *The Books and the Parchments* (Pickering, 1963)
Bruce – *Jesus and Christian Origins outside the New Testament* (H & S, 1974)
Davis (ed.) – *Cambridge History of Judaism* (Vol. 1, 1984)
Harvey – *Jesus and the Constraints of History* (Duckworth, 1982)
*Johnson – *History of the Jews* (Weidenfeld, 1987)
Metzger – *Early Versions of the New Testament* (Oxford, 1977)
Safrai (ed.) – *Jewish People in the First Century* (2 vols, Van Gorcum, 1974)

Appendix B

CHRONOLOGY OF THE PERIOD

NB: The dates relating to Jesus are of necessity conjectural

BC
63 Jerusalem captured by the Romans under Pompey
    Judaea becomes a Roman province
55 Roman invasion of Britain under Julius Caesar
37 Herod appointed 'King of the Jews'
31 Octavian (later Augustus) defeats Antony at Actium
19 Herod the Great begins reconstruction of the Temple
6   Likely date of the birth of Jesus
4   Death of Herod:
    Archelaus becomes Ethnarch of Judea
    Antipas becomes Tetrarch of Galilee
    Philip becomes Tetrarch of Iturea

AD
6   Archelaus banished. Succeeded by a Roman Governor,
    Coponius
14 Death of Augustus. Accession of Tiberius
18 Caiaphas succeeds Annas as High Priest
26 Pilate appointed Governor of Judea and Jesus begins his
    ministry in Galilee
30 The Crucifixion of Jesus
32 Martyrdom of Stephen
36 Pilate recalled to Rome
37 Death of Tiberius. Accession of Caligula
41 Death of Caligula. Accession of Claudius
43 Martyrdom of James the Apostle
44 Death of Herod Agrippa
46 First Missionary journey
48 Council of Jerusalem
49 Expulsion of the Jews from Rome
52 Felix becomes Governor of Judea

54   Death of Claudius. Accession of Nero
56   Paul imprisoned in Caesarea
59   Festus succeeds Felix as Governor
61   Death of James, the Lord's brother
64   The great fire of Rome and persecution of Christians
66   The Jewish revolt
68   The death of Nero
69   The writing of Mark's gospel
70   The fall of Jerusalem

Appendix C
THE HERODIAN DYNASTY

Antipater (Governor of Judea   47–43 BC)

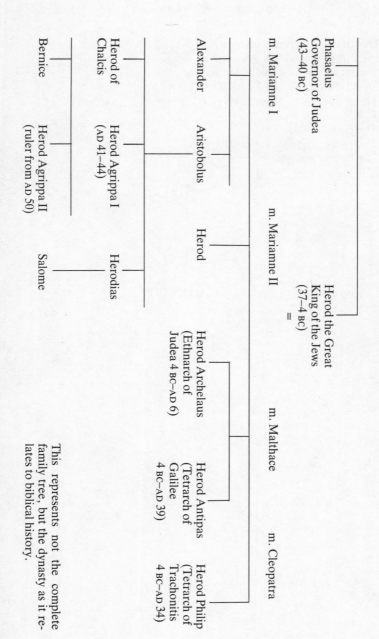

Phasaelus
Governor of Judea
(43–40 BC)

Herod the Great
King of the Jews
(37–4 BC)
=

m. Mariamne I

Alexander

Aristobolus

Herod of
Chalcis

Herod Agrippa I
(AD 41–44)

Bernice

Herod Agrippa II
(ruler from AD 50)

Salome

m. Mariamne II

Herod

Herodias

m. Malthace

Herod Archelaus
(Ethnarch of
Judea 4 BC–AD 6)

Herod Antipas
(Tetrarch of
Galilee
4 BC–AD 39)

m. Cleopatra

Herod Philip
(Tetrarch of
Trachonitis
4 BC–AD 34)

This represents not the complete
family tree, but the dynasty as it re-
lates to biblical history.

Appendix D
MAP OF PALESTINE

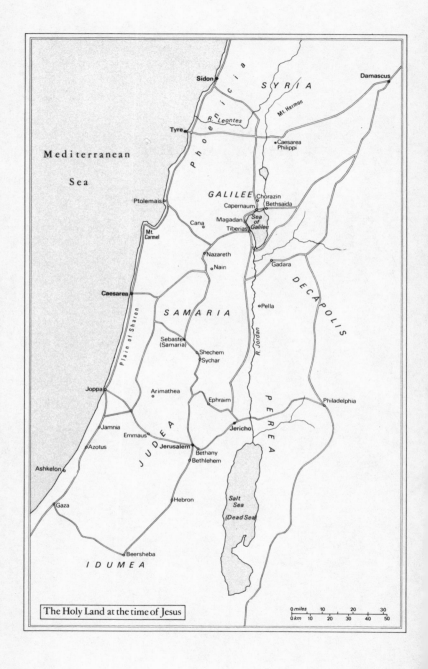

The Holy Land at the time of Jesus